Exploring
Wyre Forest & the Severn Valley

by John Roberts

WALKWAYS
by walkers...for walkers

****

WALKWAYS
John Roberts
67 Cliffe Way, Warwick
CV34 5JG   01926 776363
john@walkwaysquercus.co.uk
www.walkwaysquercus.co.uk

****

Exploring
Wyre Forest & the Severn Valley

by John Roberts

© John Roberts 2006

ISBN 0 947708 43 X

First edition 1987   ISBN 0 947708 15 4
Second edition 1991   ISBN 0 947708 25 1

a GWR pannier tank, surely the prettiest steam engine ever built

winter at Knowles Mill

the Severn in summer

Preface

DaywalkS: Wyre Forest published in 1991 gave step by step directions to a network of walks covering the whole of the Forest with some material about history, geology and so on. That book has been out of print for some years and I decided it was time to write and publish a totally new one. There was a similar book about Cannock Chase which I replaced with *Exploring Cannock Chase,* so it had to be *Exploring Wyre Forest & Severn Valley.* This will still lead you on foot to nearly every part of the Forest and to many outlying coverts, coppices and dingles, which in mediaeval times were part of a vast area of unbroken woodland. There is also a lot of up to date material on points of interest, history, geology, plants and creatures, the river, the railways and the forestry, including recent developments in forestry policy.

John Roberts

Thank you...

.. John Drewett for your immense research which appeared in *Midland Woods & Forests* and *Midland Rivers (ISBN 1 898136 01* 1994 and *08 4* (1996) which I contributed to and published. Thanks to the Worcestershire Wildlife Trust for information about plants and creatures of the forest and to Cedric Quayle who explained the strange little ponds on Walk 1b. I have drawn liberally on the books by the naturalist, Norman Hickin, *The Natural History of an English Forest* and *Wyre Forest Refreshed (ISBN 0 9505832 2* 7(1971) and *0908083 02 1* 1965), and on *The Forest is my Life* by Edwin George *(ISBN 0 86157 223 8* (1987), a professional forester. So far as I know they are out of print but they will probably be around in second hand bookshops. Publications by the Bewdley Historical Research Group were most helpful on the Bewdley and Dowles area. Finally, thank you to the writers of numberless leaflets and pamphlets published by local parishes, the county and district councils, the Severn Valley Railway and Bewdley Civic Society. Those still available can be found at the Tourist Information Centre and St Anne's Church Centre in Bewdley.

Contents

	page
Wonderful Woodland	1
Walking the Walks	2
The Forest Code	4
Beware of the Forest	4
Starting Points (and getting there)	5
Updating Service	7
General Map	9 &10
The Walks	11 - 84
Rocks and Contours	86
The River and the Streams	89
The Forest and the Trees	93
Special Trees and Special Places	97
Forest Plants and Creatures	102
Flowers, Ferns and Fungus	102
Creepers, Crawlers, Fliers and Fish	104
Deer	109
Charcoal, Bark and Coal	111
The Waterworks	115
Steam in the Woods	116

Wonderful Woodland

The ancient forest was part of the wildwood that once dominated central England. Today there is one large tract of woodland covering some 6,000 acres and there are miles of scattered coverts and small plantations that were once linked to it. Outside the woods and forests, deep, dense dingles fringe all the main streams.

The soil is mainly sandy gravel dumped onto a sandstone base some 10,000 years ago as by retreating glaciers. The predominant tree is oak but the Forestry Commission have owned the Wyre since 1925 and their planting, harvesting and replanting has been mainly of conifers. Managing for themselves are willows, birch and mountain ash. Wildlife includes dormice, fallow deer, huge wood ants, which build three foot high nests of wood fragments, and a rich variety of birds and plants.

Miles of footpaths take you through the main forest and explore the wooded fringe, through sandy valleys and up small steep hills, giving leafy glimpses of intimate corners. There are wider views from the higher, eastern bank of the river, from Shatterford, from Trimpley or nearby Wassell Wood and from the path down to the river in Walk 14 past the ruin of Nether Hollies. This hilly but mild landscape has some of the best and most varied walking in the Midlands. It is country for all seasons, with miles of misty, tossing tree tops in greens, orange, red or brown.

This is a book of walks with some information on a wide range of topics including the river, the woodlands, the animals and birds, rural industries the history of the port of Bewdley. Many books and leaflets provide more scholarly detail In Bewdley there is a bookshop, a Museum and a Tourist Information Office. At Callow Hill Forest Enterprise has a Visitor Centre.

Walking the Walks

All the walks begin at one of the eight starting points listed under **Starting Points (and getting there)**. Distances vary but the longest is Walk 10 at 16.5 kms/10 miles, and the shortest is Walk 5a at 5 kms/ 3 miles.

Some people like a longer stretch so they can link walks together. Each walk has a list of the others you can join from it; so to Walk 6 you can add Walks 1, 3, 5 and 9. Clear directions marked **OPTION** show where and how you can switch walks.

Example

You might start Walk 6 (6miles/10 kms) but at the link point switch to Walk 5 (5 miles/8.5 kms). **You would then cover the whole of Walk 5 until the directions brought you back to where you joined it** and you could resume and finish Walk 6. The total length of these walks is 11 miles/18.5 kms but you would cover 8.25 miles/14 kms because part of each walk is missed out.

I have not offered a list of possible walk combinations and distances because it would be long and complicated and I would probably get the sums wrong. Just assume that if you link walks together you will cover less than the total distance.

Long distance walkers can get a good day out because, having added one extra walk to their first choice, from that they can set out on another, and from that another. To walk the perimeter of all the walks in the book (parts of Walks 1, 3, 4, 11, 12, 16, 13, 15, 14, 8, 7 and 2) you would cover some 33 miles.

Distances in metres or miles are to give you a rough idea how far to walk. You do not need to measure because there will be something to look out for, such as a T junction or a brook. So if I say "go 1 km/.6 mile to the green fence" you will not start to wonder after 200 metres if someone has made off with it. **Distances in paces** are to be counted out.

Half R (or L) means a half turn, or about 45 degrees, *assuming you have your back to the stile, gate etc just passed.* **Bear R** (or L) means a narrower angle than a half turn, or just tending away from straight ahead. A **road** has a tarmac surface with a white line down the middle. **Lanes** are tarmac but smaller and without white lines. **Drives** are the same but not public. **Tracks** are wide enough for four wheeled vehicles and might have an earth, grass or stone surface, but not tarmac. A **path** may have any surface, from mud to tarmac, but is only pedestrian width. **Crosstracks** or **crosspaths** (single words) are like a crossroads.

If you can use a compass by all means carry it, but I don't think you will need it on these walks. The directions are drafted with great care and should be clear enough to make sure you don't get lost. *You will be fine so long as the directions seem to make sense. If, suddenly, they don't, go back to the last point at which they did and think again.* If you are still confused then most probably something has changed and if you can't work it out, go back to the start.

The **maps** are sketches to a rough scale of 2.5ins/1mile or 4cms/1km. The small numbers that appear on them refer to paragraphs in the directions.

If you want an Ordnance Survey map to help you find starting points and for general interest. Get the Explorer Map 244 (scale 1:25,000: 2.5 ins/mile or 4cms/1km.

The **map symbols** are pretty obvious but here are the main ones.

Path	· · ·· · ··	Track	- - ~ _ ~ -
Road, lane, drive	━━━	Hedge or fence	━━━<
Railway	+++++	Church	+
Stream/river/lake	~⌒~	Edge of woodland	⌒⌒
Car Park	▢	Pub	▲

3

The Forest Code
(published by the Forestry Commission)

Guard against all fires

Protect trees, plants and wildlife

Leave things as you find them, take nothing away

Keep dogs under control

Do not damage building, fences, hedges, walls and signs

Leave no litter.

Beware of the Forest

Much of the woodland on these walks is managed as commercial forest to produce crops of timber, and most of it belongs to Forest Enterprise, an offshoot of the state owned Forestry Commission. From time to time they and other managers send in crews and machines to fell or thin trees or to plant new ones. We have the right to walk through the woods on Public Footpaths and Bridleways of course, and there is also a general permission from the Forestry Commission to walk everywhere else in their woods. This permission is subject to a few clearly marked exceptions and to occasional closures to prevent walkers being nutted by falling trees or mangled in machines.

Forest Enterprise post **warning notices** around work sites. A **yellow** one just warns you that there is work going on in the area, a **red** one tells you not to climb on timber stacks while another **red** one says that a certain area is closed and you must not enter. Most often this one does not apply to the tracks people walk on but to the forest on either side. Even so, it may sometimes cover tracks (except Rights of Way), so please cooperate.

Starting Points
from south to north
(and getting there)

Bus times: 0870 6082608 or www.centro.org.uk
Severn Valley Railway: 0800 600 900 or www.svr.co.uk

Bewdley - Walk 1-1a-1b and 2.
SO 787747. The main riverside village between Stourport and Bridgnorth 3.5 miles/5 kms west of Kidderminster.
Transport and parking:
Buses. Yes.
Rail. Steam trains from Kidderminster or Bridgnorth.
Car. Parking is cheapest and easiest at Gardner's Meadow at the downstream end of the riverside street from the bridge (Severnside South).

Callow Hill - Walks 3 and 4.
SO 743739. A hilltop settlement on the A456 3 miles/5 kms west of Bewdley marked by the Royal Forester pub. NB. Do not confuse this point (where the walks start) with the Forest Visitor Centre .6 mile/1 km to the east.
Transport and parking:
Buses. Yes.
Car. Very limited street parking. Be considerate. If there is no room (eg during a service at the church) do another walk.

Buttonoak - Walks 5-5a and 9.
SO 751781. A small settlement on the B4199 3 miles/5 kms north-west of Bewdley and marked by the Button Oak pub.
Transport and parking:
Buses. Yes.
Car. Car park where the walks start, on the main road 400 yards north-west of the pub.

Upper Arley - Walks 6-6a, 7-7A, 8-8a and 10.
SO 766801. A tiny riverside village 3.7 miles/6 kms upstream of Bewdley.
Transport and parking:
Buses. Yes.
Rail. Steam trains from Kidderminster or Bridgnorth.
Car. From the east take the A442 Kidderminster – Bridgnorth road. From the west take the B4194 north-west from Bewdley. There are riverside car parks (£1) on both banks.

Kinlet Walks 11 and 12
SO 719803. A small and remote settlement at the junction of the B4194 (5.5 miles/9 kms north-west from Bewdley) and the B4363 (south from Bridgnorth).
Transport and parking:
Buses. Yes (0870 608 2608).
Car. Limited street parking. Be considerate. If there is no room for you do another walk, eg from Buttonoak 2.5 miles/4 kms south-east on the B4194.

Alveley (Severn Valley Country Park) - Walks 13, 14-14a
SO 747829 and 754840. The Country Park lies on both banks of the River Severn which are linked by a pedestrian only bridge. Alveley is on the east bank and the walks start from there.
Transport and parking:
Buses. Yes.
Rail. Steam trains from Kidderminster or Bridgnorth to Country Park Station.
Car. From the east take the A442 Kidderminster – Bridgnorth road heading for Alveley. The Park is signposted.

Hampton Loade - **Walks 15 and 16.**
SO 747865. A riverside settlement to the south-east of the Chelmarsh Reservoir.
Transport and parking:
Buses Yes (0870 608 2608) but on the east bank only for Walk 15.
Rail. Steam trains from Kidderminster or Bridgnorth.
Car. Get there from the A442 Kidderminster – Bridgnorth road. Use the car park (£1) by the river.

Updating Service

The countryside changes all the time. Paths are diverted and hedges removed, there are new tracks, fences and barns. On the Heart of England Way, for example, some 15 changes occurred in one period of three years. To keep walk directions up to date I issue Updating Slips - a unique and **free** service.

Phone or Email me (number and address on the back of the title page) with a note of the books that you have and I will send you up to date Slips. **Even new** or recently purchased books can suffer changes within weeks.

Please write, phone or email to report any changes or problems, stating book title, walk and paragraph number.

Don't bother copying changes into your book(s). Just dab affected paras with highlighter and keep the Slip in the front pocket of the plastic cover provided with it.

Many people never use this service because it's so much trouble.

westwards from Shatterford

Walk 4

Severn Valley Country Park

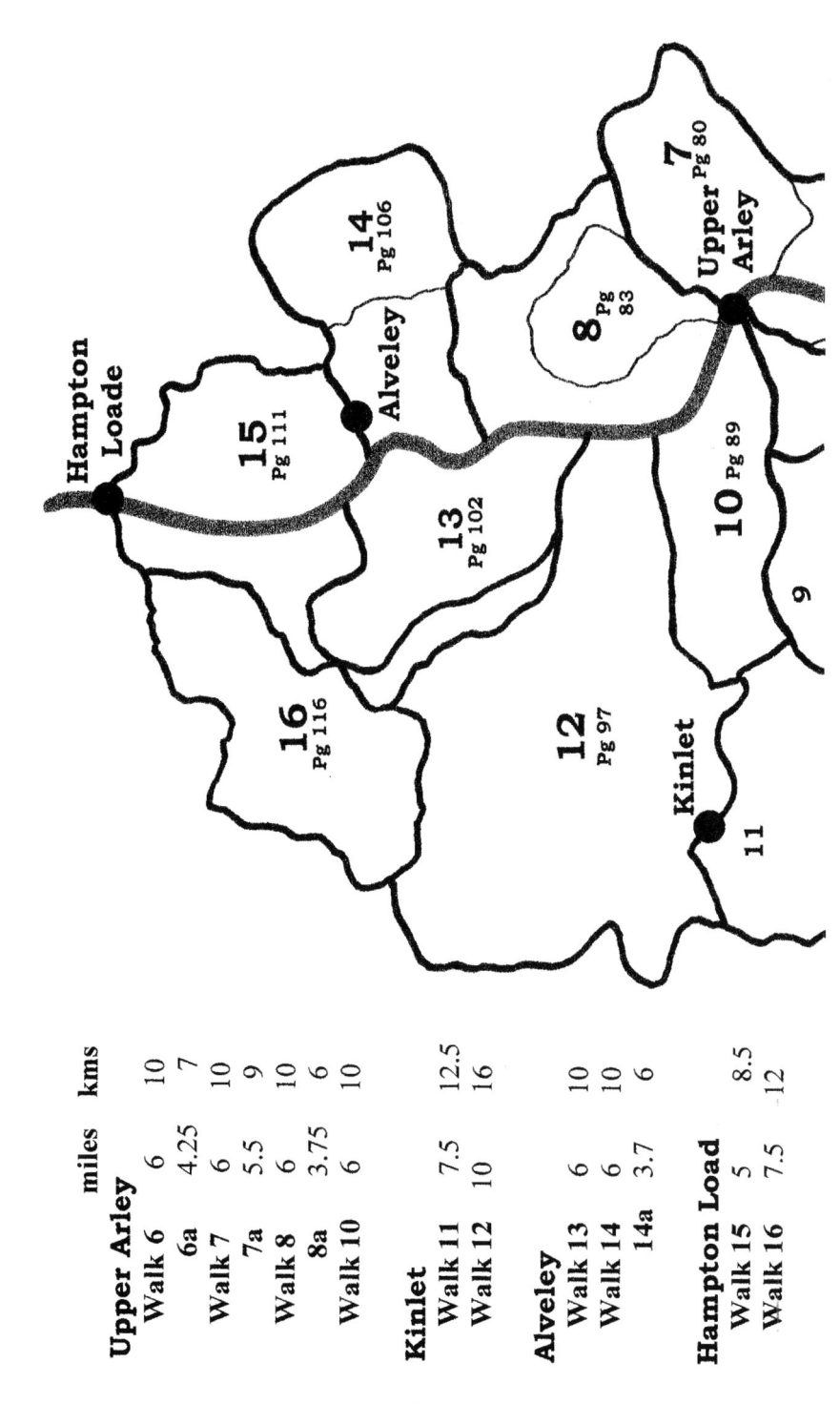

	miles	kms
Upper Arley		
Walk 6	6	10
6a	4.25	7
Walk 7	6	10
7a	5.5	9
Walk 8	6	10
8a	3.75	6
Walk 10	6	10
Kinlet		
Walk 11	7.5	12.5
Walk 12	10	16
Alveley		
Walk 13	6	10
Walk 14	6	10
14a	3.7	6
Hampton Load		
Walk 15	5	8.5
Walk 16	7.5	12

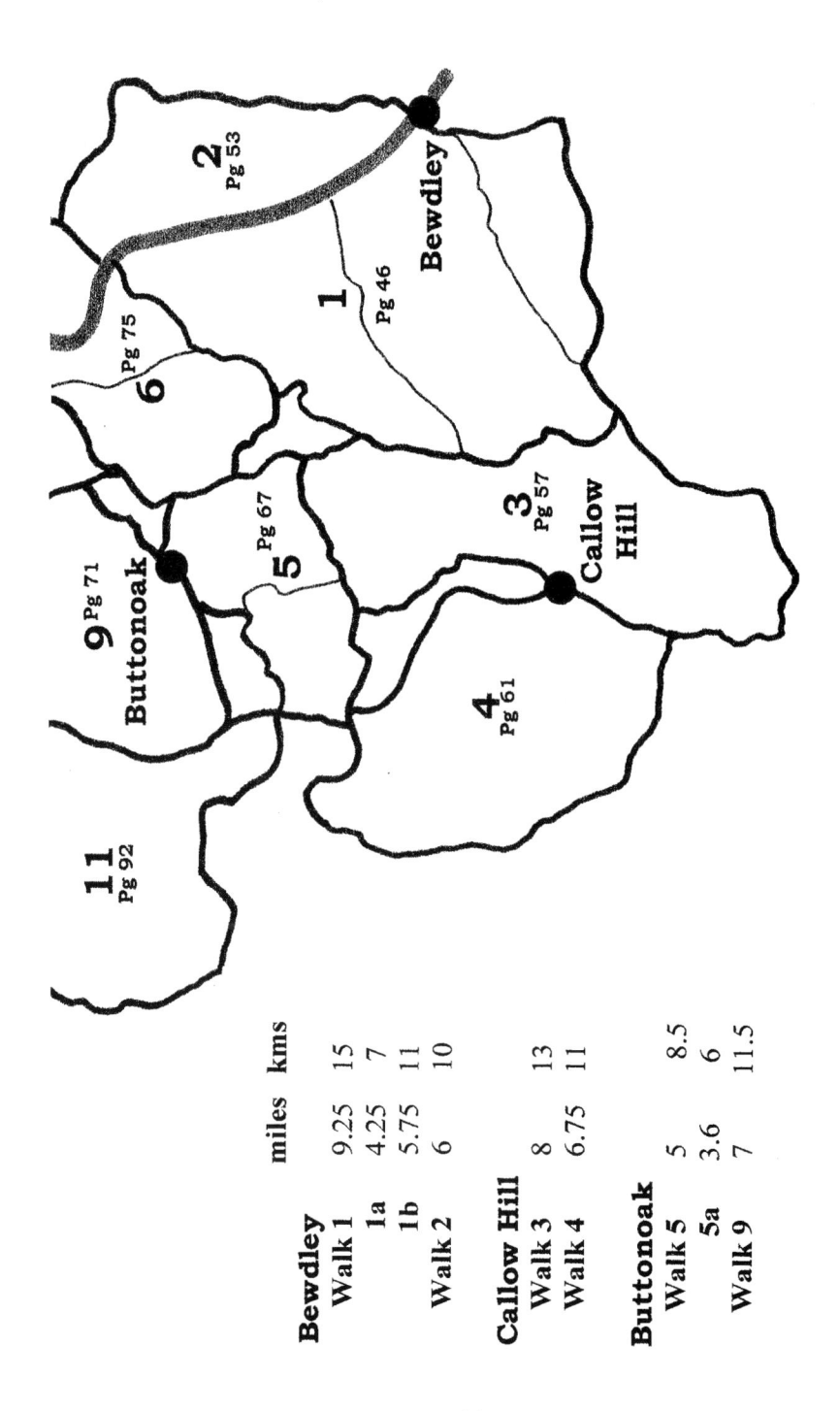

	miles	kms
Bewdley		
Walk 1	9.25	15
1a	4.25	7
1b	5.75	11
Walk 2	6	10
Callow Hill		
Walk 3	8	13
Walk 4	6.75	11
Buttonoak		
Walk 5	5	8.5
5a	3.6	6
Walk 9	7	11.5

Bewdley
(Walks 1-1a-1b and 2)

The town spreads for about a mile in each direction but the centre is a compact huddle of handsome buildings, timber framed, red brick or creamy sandstone. The main street sweeps around the baroque church of St Anne (1695 and 1745), on its island, and swirls gently down to cross the river by Telford's stone bridge (1789). The individual structures are delightful, the church, the bridge, the Guild Hall (1808) and the old Post Office (16th century) next to it, but every building, kink and passage contribute to this near perfect Georgian town. Look along Severnside South with its buildings of all heights, assorted windows, doors, porches, hoods, canopies and graceful cast iron balconies. Look down High Street for some very fine timber framed houses. From the Tourist Information Centre, from Bewdley Books and in the church you can find leaflets and booklets, including a history of Bewdley and a Town Trail.

Bewdley was a port on the Severn when the river was the best link between the Midlands and Bristol and the sea. Edward VI granted the town a Royal Charter in 1472 and started a prosperous trade in leather, skins, wax, corn, timber and coal, and later cotton, tobacco, sugar and tea. Then there was boat building, rope making, bass founding and pewtering. In 1539 the chronicler, John Leyland, wrote *".. at the rysyng of the sunne from est the hole town gliterith, being all of new buyldinge, as it wer of gold."*. This ended after Bewdley rejected a plan to make it a terminus for the Staffordshire & Worcestershire Canal and trade shifted to the specially built Stourport on Severn.

Walks 1-1a and 1b

Starting point: all walks start from the tower of St Anne's church at a door on the UPPER side.
Lengths: Walk 1 - 8.5 miles/14 kms, 1a - 4.5 miles/7.5 kms, 1b - 6.7 miles /11 kms.
Walks you can join: Walks 3 and 6.
Refreshments: lots of cafes and pubs at the start but nothing on the way round.

Walk 1. A woodland start from Bewdley to Ribbesford Woods, then a steep climb for wide and leafy views over the Severn Valley. Several miles of dreamy oak woods take you down to the Dowles Brook then a gentle rise through spruce and Scots pine to level off before a steep fall to river level. The last section follows the River Severn.

Walk 1a is a pleasant short cut back to Bewdley which crosses a golf course and a high point, giving heart lifting views over the Severn.

Walk 1b takes to a deep and secret little valley lined with tall oaks, some very old Scots pine, a few very large Wellingtonia and a dense mass of rhododendrons. There is yew and ash and bilberry, with iris by the small, bright brook. It has been dammed in several places to form to form scenic pools but they are now overgrown and silted so that the valley seems lost and forgotten.

The walk follows the **Worcestershire Way** for the first couple of miles. This 40 mile/75 kms trail used to run from Kinver Edge on the western fringe of the West Midlands to the southern tip of the Malvern Hills but was recently truncated to start at Bewdley. With these intricate and alluring Worcestershire hills and their woods and streams, this is the most scenic of the Long Distance Paths in this area.

St Leonard's, Ribbesford, is a modest rural church with a pleasing timber bell turret and a pretty white porch marked 1633. The stone of the tympanum, or panel, over the church door is

St Leonard's Ribbesford

now horribly worn but the carving shows a hunter riding a space hopper while shooting a bagpipe. The timber columns and arches to the south aisle are 15th century and the only ones in Worcestershire. Look for the fragments of mediaeval stained glass worked into the south-west window, the south window by Burne Jones and the carving on the pulpit and lectern.

Knowles Mill is one of four surviving mills on the Dowles Brook. Town Mill and Furnace Mill have been altered and converted to private houses while Cooper's Mill has been rebuilt as a youth outdoor centre. However, Knowles is owned by the National Trust and has been kept very much as it was in its working days. The modest stone buildings seem restful and content.

(1) Put your back to St Anne's church tower doorway & cross road into Park Lane opposite. Go 50 mtrs (past public bench) & take rising brick path L.

(2) Take iron gate, ignore R fork, go 150 mtrs & fork R. Go 100 mtrs & join stone path (Worcs Way).

(3) Go ahead, cross stream & take small gate. Go ahead by R fence [CHECK] to meet stone track. Go 250 mtrs & take gate onto lane.

(4) Take track opposite, pass R fork & go under A456. Go 300 mtrs to pass farm L & take church gate.

(5) Follow path past porch & take rising path R. Go through stone gateway, cross stile L & climb upfield path to seat.

(6) Follow woodland path 300 mtrs & cross stile into field. Go ahead to gate & cross stile. Follow path to drive & go L to lane.

(7) Go L 50 mtrs & take earth track R (leaving Worcs Way). Go through woodland to field. Go R around field edge, pass 1st waymark post & at 2nd turn R & join woodland path.

(8) Go 600 mtrs/.4 mile to wood corner & cross stile into field.

(9) Cross stile L & follow fenced path to driveway. Go R 350 mtrs to Outdoor Centre entrance & take track R.

(10) Go 250 mtrs (past brick building) & follow wooded track to fork with iron gate L.

(11) Go R & meet track. Go L 250 mtrs to track junction near machine shed.

Folley Point

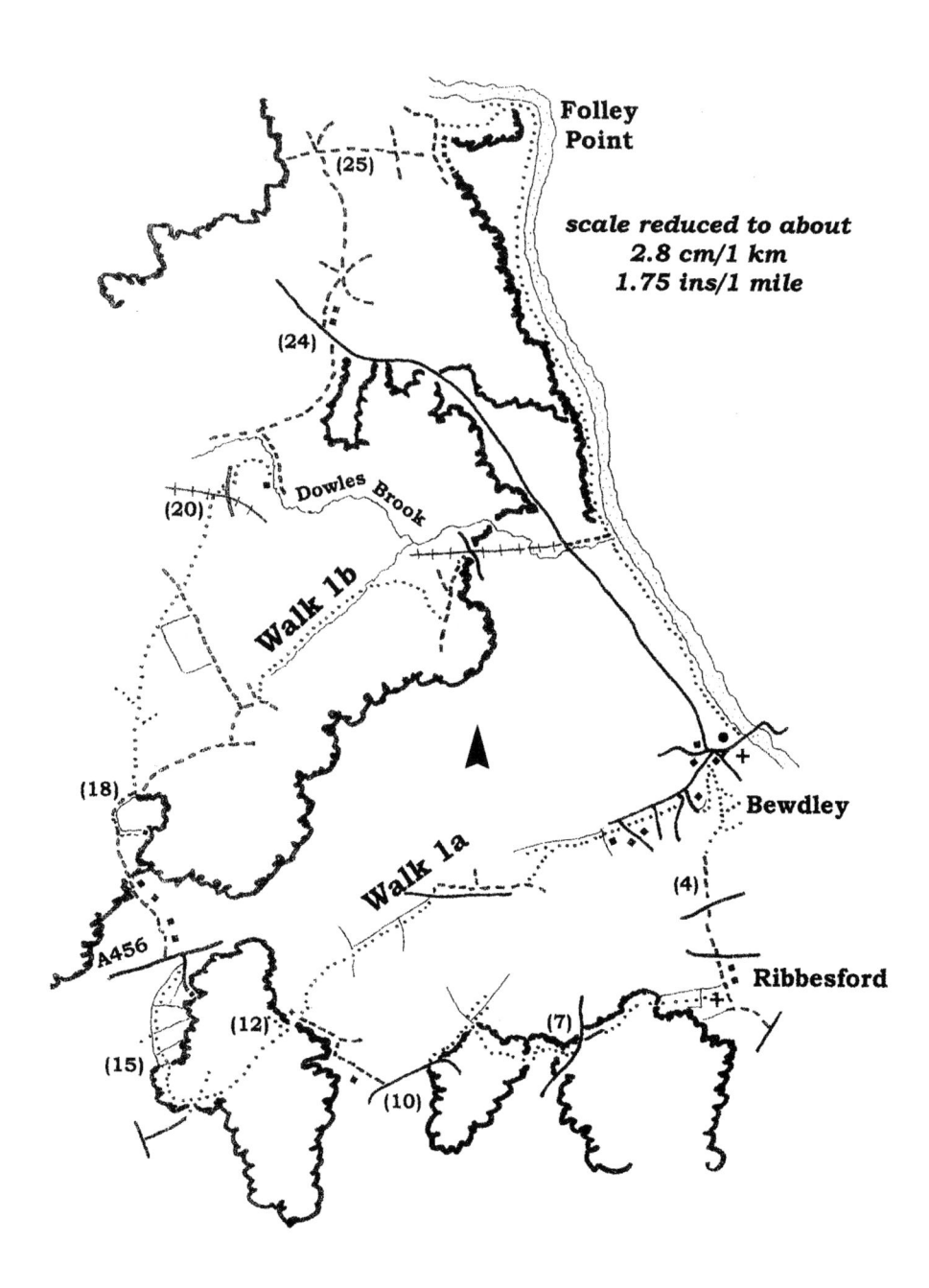

scale reduced to about
2.8 cm/1 km
1.75 ins/1 mile

(25)

(24)

Dowles Brook

(20)

Walk 1b

(18)

Bewdley

Walk 1a

(4)

A456

Ribbesford

(15) (12)

(7)

(10)

****

OPTION

To continue Walk 1 go to para (12). **To finish Walk 1a** see below.

(1a1) Go R to meet tarmac path. Go L to its end then turn ½ R to gap between hillocks, & find waymark post. [Post revolves so ignore direction of arrows.]

(1a2) Pass bunker close on your L & keep this line to find waymark post in trees. Turn ½ R & pass bunker close on your R to reach tree clump with track running ahead.

(1a3) Follow track past ponds & waymark post, then keep same line to hilltop tree ahead & find waymark post. Keep same line through grass & trees (with tee on your L) heading for gate under oak, & cross stile.

(1a4) Go parallel with L fence to gate & cross stile. Go L & cross stile onto A456. **GREAT CARE**. Cross road & take stile to join stone track.

(1a5) Go around R bend & on for 700 mtrs/.4 mile (past waymark post) up to group of young trees L.

(1a6) Bear ½ L off stone track to pass tree clump close on your L & follow faint grass track to hill crest. Go with young trees on your L, then parallel with wire fence & take gap.

(1a7) Follow track 10 paces then go ½ L across grass to hill crest. Follow field edge to corner & cross stile.

(1a8] Follow fenced path to road. Take path opposite to lane. Go L a few paces, cross lane & take walled path to road. Go L to T junction.

(1a9) Go R a few paces & take rising lane R up to L bend. Pass wooden gate & cross stile. Follow fenced path (over stile & past path R) to meet path from R. Take iron gate to road. Go L back to start.
****

main Walk 1 continues

(12) Go L, pass track R & follow woodland path 500 mtrs to path junction on wood edge.

(13) Go R to meet path, then go L a few paces to notice board on wood corner.

****
OPTION
To join Walk 3 go ahead to tarmac drive, go R 300 mtrs to road then turn to Walk 3 para 15.
****

(14) Go R on woodland path around wood edge & cross stile into field.

(15) Follow L hedge/fence through 3 fields & cross stile onto driveway. Go L to A456. **GREAT CARE**.

(16) Cross road, go L 100 mtrs & take St John's Lane R. Follow stone track 700 mtrs/.4 mile to its end at two gates.

(17) Pass L gate & take path 250 mtrs (past path L) to fork by notice board.

****
OPTION
To continue Walk 1 go to para (18). **To finish Walk 1b** see below.

(1b1) Fork R, follow woodland track 500 mtrs (past 2 small paths L) & take track L.

(1b2) Go 350 mtrs to meet bend of stone track. Go R 100 paces to track L. Follow it 7 paces then take small, steep path R.

(1b3) Go 1.2 kms/.7 mile down valley bottom staying near stream. **Watch** for an octagonal brick tank thing in stream & cross next dam/causeway R.

(1b4) Follow rising track & cross a track to reach T junction. Go L down main track to gate & car park. Go L to lane.

(1b5) Cross bearing L & take steps up to old railway. Follow to its end then go down to B4119. **GREAT CARE.**

(1b6) Don't cross here. Go R 100 mtrs then cross to gate & take stile. Follow track to river.

(1b7) Go R 1.3 kms/.8 mile to Bewdley.
****

main Walk 1 continues
(18) Fork L & follow track 600 mtrs/.35 mile, then pass 1st path R, round L bend & take 2nd path R.

(19) Go 500 mtrs & meet track. Cross & keep ahead on possibly faint track (nb wire fences at 10 mtrs each side). Pass pool R & join track from R. Go ahead 50 paces, take path R & cross stile.

(20) Follow grass path to cross stile & bridge. Go on & cross stile onto drive. Turn ½ R & cross stile into field. Go ½ L down to cross stile.

(21) Go 7 paces, then take path L & curve down to mill. Cross footbridge to reach track.

(22) Go L 450 mtrs to within sight of gate with rising track R.

****
OPTION
To join Walk 6 go ahead through gate plus 150 metres to stone track. Turn to Walk 6 para 9.
****

(23) Go R 850 mtrs (past tracks L & R) & take double wooden gates onto B4199. **GREAT CARE.**

(24) Cross, go L on verge 100 mtrs & take drive/track R. Go 400 mtrs to track junction & take 2nd track L behind pole barrier. Go 600 mtrs/.35 mile to brick thingys.

(25) Go R down grass ride 600 mtrs/.35 mile to next brick thingy & turn L.

(26) Follow stone track past bungalows & take 1st path R (by waymark post) down to river.

(27) Cross stile R & follow riverside path 4 kms/2.5 miles back to Bewdley.

Walk 2

Starting point: the town centre side of the river bridge.
Length: - 6 miles/10 kms.
Walks you can join: Walk 7.
Refreshments: lots of cafes and pubs at the start but nothing on the way round.

The long stroll by the river is easy and interesting, then comes a steep climb through woodland and along a lane lasting almost a mile. The rest is a long descent to the Severn with wide and glorious views. From these high fields the first sweeping panorama is of fields and woods dipping to the Severn then rising to the long, uneven hump of the Abberley Hills. Further left is the more alpine outline of the Malverns. Later you can see Titterstone and Brown Clee Hills.

The **Bewdley to Leominster Railway** crossed the river about three quarters of a mile upstream from Bewdley and the piers are still standing. Read about it under "Steam in the Woods". The strange combination of blue brick and buff sandstone is not beautiful and the piers are ungainly, but the workmanship is superb.

The massive steelwork of the **Elan Valley Aqueduct** is impressive from a distance but close to it is overwhelming. Crossing the river was a huge work but tunnelling through the steep hillside on the east bank caused the engineer a lot more trouble because of unstable, sandy ground. (See "The Waterworks".)

Trimply Reservoirs provide water from the Severn to the local area. They are a fine place on a summer's day to combine fishing or a picnic with steam train watching.

(1) From town centre end of Bewdley bridge, cross river & turn L past Bridge House. Follow drive past rowing club up to gate (not through it) & take fenced path L to river.

(2) Go R on riverside paths 2 kms/1.25 miles (past water tower and old railway bridge) to field with redbrick 2 storey house. Keep fence on your L & cross stile to lane.

(3) Go L 200 mtrs to phone box & take track L down to cattle grid. Go R 800 mtrs/.5 mile to end of field at chalet "Rendevous", & take path R to stile & track.

(4) Go L on track & riverside paths 600 mtrs/.4 mile, then cross stile to fingerpost & information board.

****
OPTION
To join Walk 7 continue by river to Arley bridge then turn to Walk 7 para (1).
****

(5) Go R up to reservoir, walk R around it to railway gate, & cross line.

(6) Go ahead then fork R. Go 100 mtrs to fingerpost L & turn sharp R. Follow path past white gates plus 300 mtrs to wood edge gate, & cross stile to field.

(7) Go parallel with L fence to wide gap, then keep ahead past hedge corner & cross stile onto track. Go up to road.

Trimpley Reser'vs

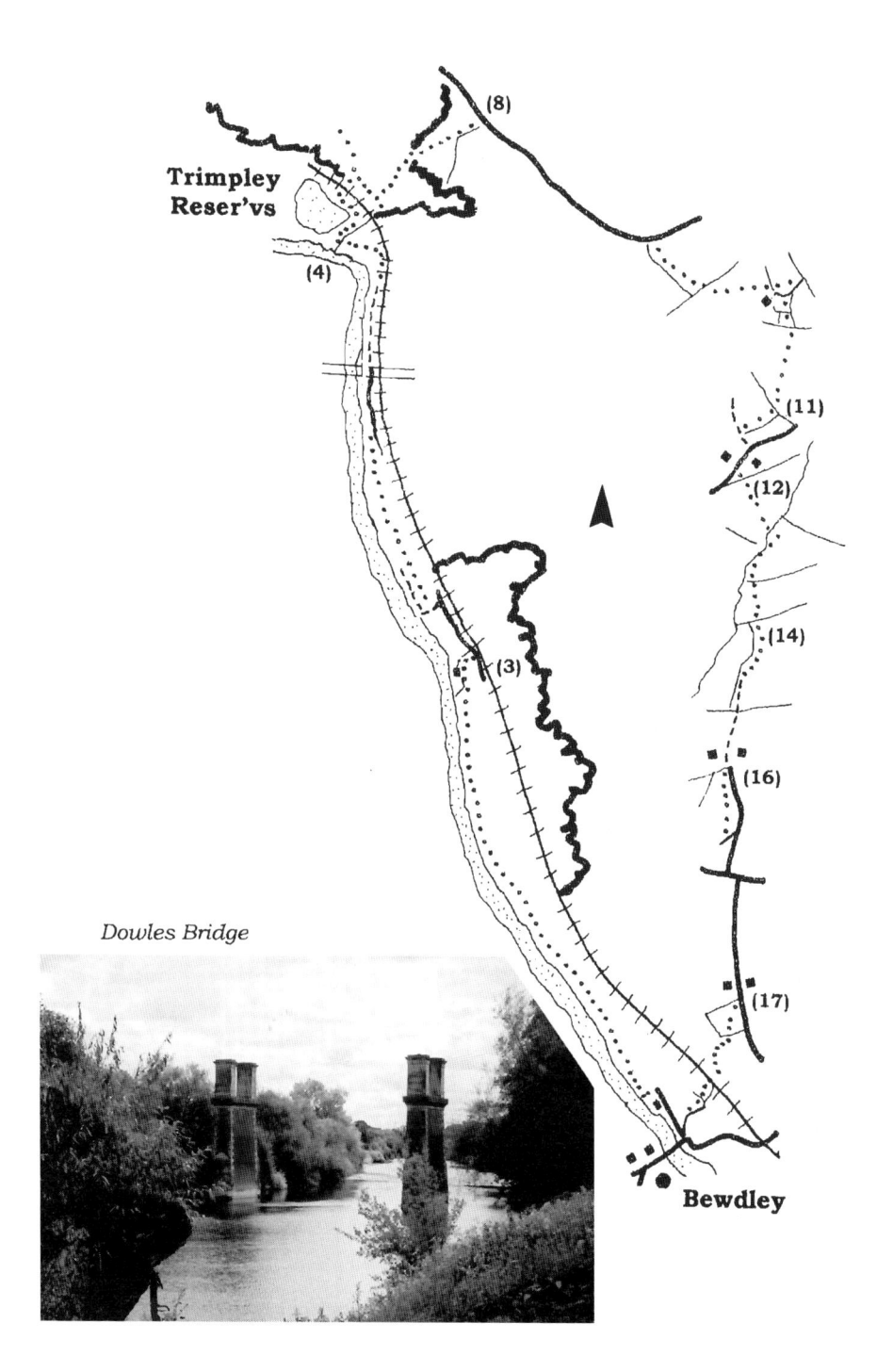

Dowles Bridge

Bewdley

21

(8) Go R 1 km/.6 mile to layby R, & at its far end cross stile.

(9) Go parallel with R fence & (when in view) head for far gate & cross stile. Go ½ L to L side of farm & cross stile. Cross stile ahead then keep same line to stile & drive.

(10) Go R to R bend then ½ L to cross stile. Cross field diagonally & take stile. Keep this line over midfence stile to wood & cross stile into field.

(11) Go ahead down field edge to track & turn L to lane. Go R 100 mtrs to gate of "Hawthornes" & cross stile L. Go R by hedge & cross stile.

(12) Follow power poles but bear L to find concealed stile into trees, & go through to field.

(13) Go R down field edge & cross stile. Follow power lines but head 20 mtrs R of next pylon to cross concealed stile.

(14) Go R by hedge/fence to gate & cross stile to green track. Go ahead via 2 gates & pass farm to drive.

(15) Follow drive to bungalow & cross stile R. Cross field diagonally & take stile. Keep ahead to gate & cross stile onto lane.

(16) Go ahead & pass lane R to road junction. Go R 450 mtrs/.25 mile to pass pink shed & cross stile R.

(17) Go ½ L up to field corner & cross stile onto hedged path. Go R 150 mtrs & cross railway. **GREAT CARE.**

(18) Cross lane & take steps to field. Follow L hedge, take gates & follow hedged path to drive. Go L to start.

Callow Hill
(Walks 3 and 4)

This small settlement on the edge of the forest is no more than a pub, a tiny Methodist Church and some houses, but the heavily wooded and secretive landscape conceals a surprising number of scattered houses and cottages. Many local people can trace their families back for centuries in this area when their ancestors followed the forest crafts of timber cutting, charcoal burning, barking for tanning leather, besom and basket making. The Royal Forester inn is said to the oldest in Worcestershire, though it was previously called Mopson's Cross.

Walk 3

Starting point: from the Methodist Church. To find it take the A456 from Bewdley for 5 miles/3 kms to the Royal Forester pub and turn right. Roadside parking only and space is very limited. If it is crowded (eg Sunday) do another walk.
Length: 8 miles/13 kms.
Walks you can join: Walks 5, 1 and 1b.
Refreshments: the Royal Forester at the start.

The walk starts on long tracks that curve and dip through the forest, a popular place for family cycling. The woodland is mainly conifers with a trackside fringe of oaks and ground cover of grasses, bracken and brambles. In places there is bilberry and heather, suggesting an acid soil. Next comes the Dowles Brook, shrouded in trees and sometimes invisible from the track, then higher, lighter oakwoods. Two thirds of this walk is through forest but the rest runs through small field and woods and past scattered farms, with some steep climbs up hillsides and drops into deep dingles.

(1) From Methodist Church walk away from A456 & follow lane to its end. Go ahead into wood. Pass side paths R & L & follow line of cypress trees to corner of block where path forks.

(2) Take middle of 3 paths & go 200 mtrs to stone track with seat.

(3) Go L 1.5 kms/1 mile to junction with finger post.

(4) Go L 500 mtrs/.3 mile to crosstracks with finger post.

(5) Go ahead 450 mtrs/.25 mile to cross Dowles Brook.

****
OPTION
To join Walk 5 *turn L* & go to Walk 5 para 9; distance is only 1.5 kms/.9 mile.
****

(6) Go R by brook 400 mtrs/.25 mile to track junction. Go ahead across small brook & turn R.

(7) Cross Dowles Brook, go 700 mtrs/.4 mile to markpost with horseshoe, & take rising earth track R.

(8) Go 200 mtrs to meet track. Go L to junction of stone tracks by finger post. Go L 200 mtrs & take gate R.

(9) Follow rising earth track 550 mtrs/.3 mile passing tracks R & L into reedy area, to meet paths R & L with waymarks on trees.

****
OPTION
To join Walk 1 *go L* & turn to Walk 1 para 19 line 2.
****

(10) Go R & follow woodland path 1 km/.6 mile (past fenced grassland L & joining track from R) to path junction by signboard.

****
OPTION
To join Walk 1b *fork L*, turn to Walk 1 end of para 17, then para 1b1, starting from " ...follow...".
****

25

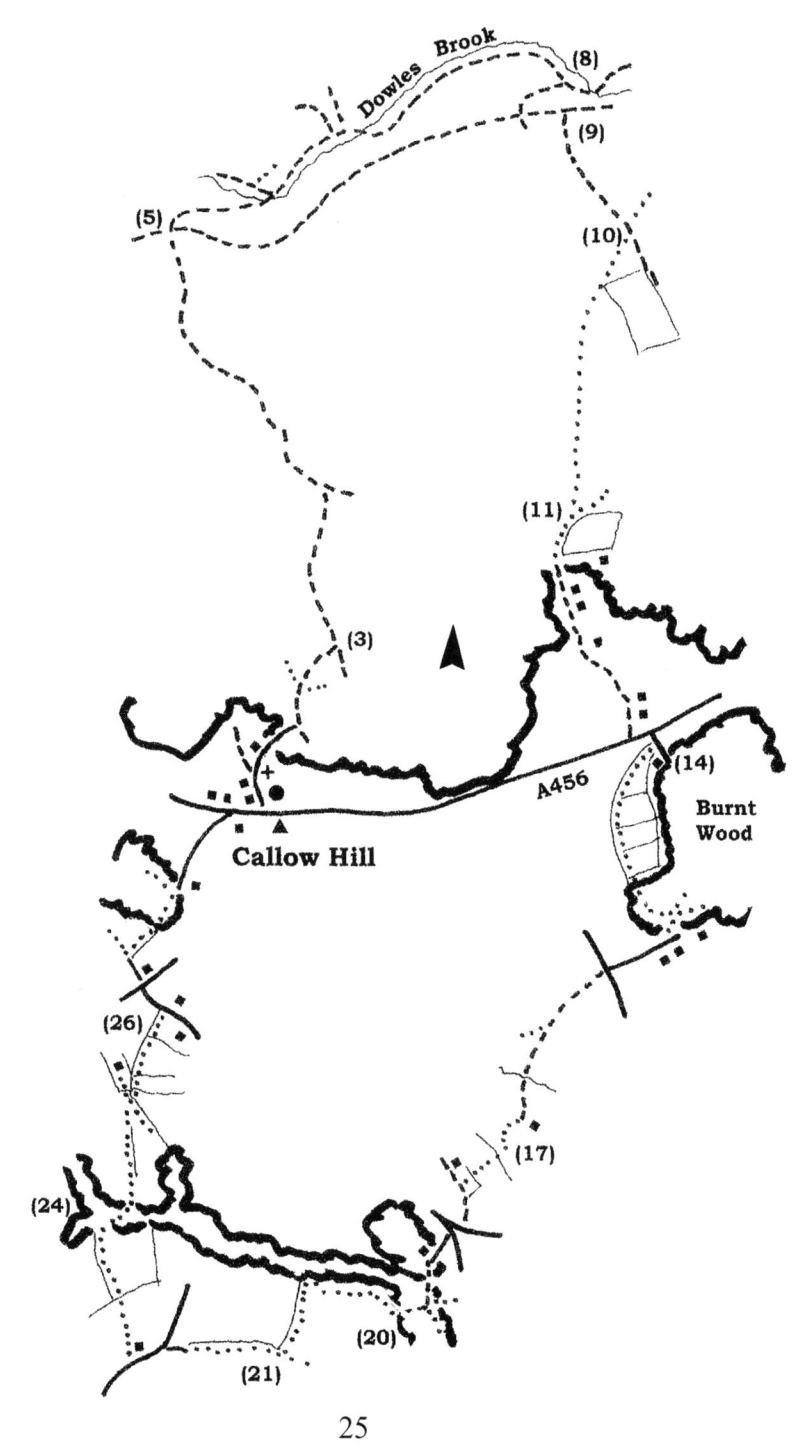

(11) Go ahead & follow path by field to gate & track. Go ahead 1 km/.6 mile to A456. **CARE**.

(12) Don't cross here. Go L 80 mtrs then cross into tarmac drive (Tarn). Go ahead through gateway then R to cross stile.

(13) Follow R hedge 700 mtrs/.4 mile via 2 gates/stile & cross stile into wood.

(14) Follow path around wood edge to meet path by markpost. Go R to tarmac drive then R 300 mtrs to road.

(15) Cross bearing L & take gate. Follow hedged track 400 mtrs (ignore yellow arrow L) & cross footbridge.

(16) Follow path, pass house, follow green track 120 mtrs to L bend & take rusty gate. Enter field, follow R hedge & take gate, then cross stile.

(17) Go ahead to pass holly tree close on your L. Keep this line towards white house but bear L to pass end of ragged hedge L, & cross stile. Cross garden & take stile onto stone track.

(18) Go L 150 mtrs to road. Go R a few paces & take lane L. Follow it 50 mtrs & take gated drive R.

(19) Go to double trunked oak & turn L to cross stile. Follow R fence & cross 2 stiles into woodland. Follow path & cross stile onto green track. Go R to meet track.

(20) Go L & cross brook. Go R through hedge gap & follow fenced track to end of L fence. Follow field edge 400 mtrs (past falling track R) to field corner. Go up by R hedge to projecting hedge corner.

(21) Go R by hedge to field corner & cross stile. Follow R fence/hedge through 1st gate & 2nd, then follow green track & take gate. Go R & take small gate onto lane.

(22) Go L 200 mtrs to pass farm & cross stile R. Follow R fence & go to far end of barn. Go ahead to double gates & cross stile on their R.

(23) Follow L hedge down to bottom field corner, then go R by trees 30 mtrs & cross footbridge.

(24) Enter field & look L to see two midfield trees. Head for L one then go with trees on your R to their end. Bear R to hedge then find stile by markpost. Don't cross yet.

****
OPTION
To join Walk 4 *go L* by hedge 20 mtrs, then turn to Walk 4 para 5 from ".... cross ...."
****

(25) Cross stile, go half L across field corner & take stile. Follow L hedge past gap & over 3 stiles to lane. Go L 100 mtrs to T junction.

(26) Cross lane, take R of 2 drives & cross stile. Turn R down hedge to field corner & cross stile into wood. Follow path to wood corner & cross stile.

(27) Go ahead & join lane to A456. **CARE**. Cross here, go R & take 1st lane L back to start.

Walk 4

Starting point: from the Methodist Church. To find it take the A456 from Bewdley for 5 miles/3 kms to the Royal Forester pub and turn right. Roadside parking only and space is very limited. If it is crowded (eg Sunday) do another walk.
Length: 6.75 miles/11 kms.
Walks you can join: Walk 5.
Refreshments: the Royal Forester at the start and the Horse & Jockey when you meet the A4117.

WARNING: The first 250 metres of the path by the Dowles Brook is very rewarding but it is rocky and steep and can be difficult where there are no handholds. Go and see, but if you feel you can't manage it go back and follow the alternative by lanes, as shown in the directions.

The first half of the walk crosses an intricate landscape of steep, heavily wooded valleys with a procession of glorious views. From the highest point you have a full panorama; to the north are the spiky outlines of conifers in the Wyre Forest. To the east and south the gentle roundness of oaks rises and falls to the horizon, while to the west is the barren hump of Titterstone Clee. The northern half of the walk runs through light and airy oakwood, but there is a picturesque passage along a small gorge of the Dowles Brook.

(1) From Methodist church head for A456. Don't cross here. Go R on footway 180 mtrs to opposite house with double gable ends. (CARE) Cross road into drive on its R.

(2) Walk to end of tarmac then go ahead on earth track & cross stile into wood. Go a few paces to bend of path, fork L for 200 mtrs & cross stile into field.

(3) Follow L hedge to pass last house & cross stile L. Go ahead to lane junction. Go ahead 100 mtrs & cross stile R into garden.

(4) Follow R hedge & cross stiles 1 and 2. Pass gap R & go on to cross corner stile in bushes. Turn ½ R & cross stile.

(5) Turn R, follow hedge 20 mtrs & cross stile into garden. Go ahead & takes gates then follow drive to road junction.

(6) Go L to end of tarmac then follow stone track 100 mtrs & cross stile R.

(7) Follow woodland path & exit to field. Go L, follow edge of cultivated area to meet bottom fence & take gap by waymarked tree. Cross planks & stile into field.

(8) Go R on field edge 400 mtrs (past stile) to tarmac drive.

(9) Go R to A456. CARE. Cross here, go L on verge 130 mtrs to pass water tower & take lane R.

(10) Go 50 mtrs & take stone track R. Go 400 mtrs & cross cattle grid. Bear L to cross stile.

(11) Go R by garden wall, then hedge, for 250 mtrs & cross stile R. Go L between hedge & shed, then follow L hedge (past stile) to stile & lane junction.

(12) Go ahead 200 mtrs (past 3 houses) & take track L.

(13) Go 100 mtrs to near gate then bear L off track & follow L hedge down to cross stile. Go ahead by R hedge (as near as undergrowth permits) to bottom R field corner, & cross stile onto lane.

(14) Go R & round R bend to T junction. Go R to next bend, then go ahead to gate & cross stile on its R.

(15) Go ahead past track L & take rising path to cross stile. Follow path up through wood & cross stile into field.

(16) Go ahead & cross stile, then cross field diagonally to enter tunnel of trees & cross 2 stiles. Follow R hedge & cross 2 stiles to A4117. **CARE**.

(17) Cross to track opposite & take gate. Go ahead & take gate onto stone track. Go 300 mtrs to L bend by 2 bar black fence. Go on 120 paces to bridleway sign & take path L.

(18) Go 400 mtrs to wooden barriers. Pass through & take path beyond for 270 mtrs to meet track. Go R down to old railway.

(19) Go ahead through barrier & follow path up to track. Go ahead 12 paces & cross stile L. Follow R fence to bottom field corner & take gate.

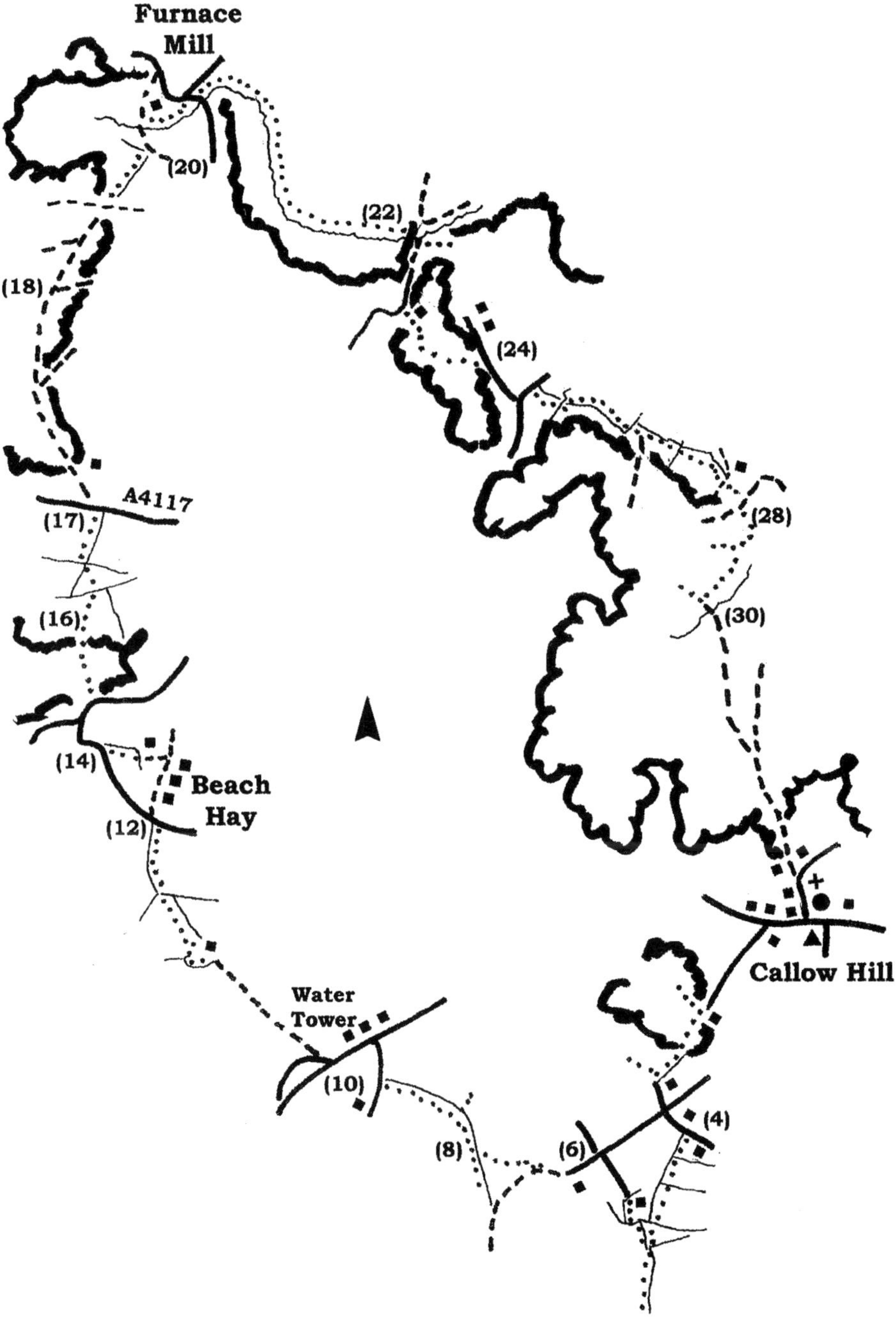
Furnace Mill
(20)
(22)
(18)
(24)
A4117
(17)
(28)
(16)
(30)
(14)
Beach Hay
(12)
Callow Hill
Water Tower
(10)
(4)
(8)
(6)

(20) Go ahead to drive, go L 75 mtrs & cross stile R behind bank. Follow drive to iron gates & take kissing gate on their L to lane. Go R 20 paces then cross & take path L.

[20A] Note the warning above. If you don't care for the Dowles Brook path return to this lane and:

    (a) Follow lane over bridge, go 500 mtrs & turn L.
    (b) Go 700 mtrs to junction & take lane ahead.
    (c) Go 100 mtrs to house & turn to para (23).

(21) Follow up & down path by Dowles Brook for 1 km/.6 mile to steel bridge. *(CARE –first 250 mtrs is rocky & steep in places. Later path swings L away from brook to cross stepping stones but continues through conifers & rejoins brook. Stay by brook by going R at forks.)*

****
OPTION
To join Walk 5 *turn L* up rising track then go to Walk 5 para 10 starting at "...800 mtrs...".
****

(22) Cross bridge, go R to cross small footbridge & take rising track 300 mtrs to house L.

(23) Take gate beside it & follow R hedge onto wooded track. Go down to cross small brook then up L 250 mtrs to tarmac drive.

(24) Go R 200 mtrs to lane. Go L 50 mtrs & cross stile R. Follow L hedge to field corner & cross stile. Take fenced path to stile & field.

(25) Go R by hedge/fence to field corner, cross stile & go L to track. (If obstructed take gate onto track.) Follow track 28 paces & turn L through L of two gates.

(26) Follow R fence for 28 paces & cross stile R. Go on down fence to field corner, take steps & cross plank.

(27) Cross stile & follow fenced path to cross stile. Follow woodland path to track. Cross stile opposite, follow woodland path & cross stile onto earth track.

(28) Go R 10 mtrs to R bend & turn L. Follow path round R curve to Y junction of wide paths by waymarked tree.

(29) Go L 300 mtrs (past paths R & L) & down to cross brook by plank (may be bust).

(30) Take rising path ahead 600 mtrs/.4 mile to track junction. Go R to edge of wood & follow stone track via gate/stile onto lane. Go R to start.

Walk 6

Knowles Mill on the Dowles Brook

Buttonoak
(Walks 5 and 9)

This settlement in the middle of the forest spreads further than you might think, but not much. The agreeable pub with its garden has ancient origins and some wattle and daub has been found in a wall. There is a village shop built on the site of a Methodist chapel, a school converted to a dwelling and a cluster of stone or brick houses with timber houses for forestry workers.

Buttonoak was a centre for charcoal burning and the name may come from "boothen", plural of booth, which was the tepee like shelter a burner lived in during the five or so days it took his mound to burn. Local people practised all the other forest crafts and for more about them see "Charcoal, Bark & Coal". They also kept pigs, sheep and cows which roamed in the woodland and often wore bells so they could be found. Cottage orchards supplied cherries, damsons, pears and apples for cider making; you will find their remains all around.

Walks 5 and 5a
Starting point: from the car park .4 west of the Button Oak pub.
Length: Walk 5 – 5.2 miles/8.5 kms, Walk 5a –3.6 miles/6 kms.
Walks you can join: Walks 6, 3, 4, 11 and 9.
Refreshments: the Button Oak.

To many people all conifer trees look like bog brushes but there are many species. Some of those on the first mile of this walk are Western hemlock, a forest tree from North America with foliage rather like our native yew. The six trunked oak by the grassy ride started life with the usual single stem but was coppiced; the girth of the new trunks shows that it has not been cut for many years. Look out for sandy banks of beautiful heathers and bilberry. There is a long stretch by the Dowles Brook and a walk through one of the quiet and remote clearings in the woodland. Few of these walks are entirely within the forest but 5a is, following beautiful paths and tracks through the oaks and conifers

(1) From car park pass pole barrier, go 12 paces & take small path L to T junction. Go L & through damp patch to junction. Go L by fence 500 mtrs to bottom of wide grass ride.

****
OPTION
To join Walk 6 take gate L, follow L fence & cross stile onto B4199. Turn to Walk 6 para 13.
****

(2) Go ahead on stone track 500 mtrs/.3 mile, pass stone track L up to earth track R, then go on 50 paces to fork.

(3) Go ahead/L, pass falling track L & go 750 mtrs/.5 mile to junction with path R & falling track L.

(4) Go L to junction. Go L to brookside track. Go R & cross footbridge.

(5) Go R up to crest then down to brook level. Cross small stream & take hollow track ahead to meet rising track L.

****
OPTION
To join Walk 3 *turn L* & go to Walk 3 para 8.
****

(6) Go ahead 1km/.6 mile & cross bridge to track junction.

(7) Go L, pass track R & go 350 mtrs to junction before bridge.

(8) Go R by Dowles Brook 130 mtrs to short markpost with blue arrows & small path R.

****
OPTION
To continue Walk 5 go to para (8). **To finish Walk 5a** see below.

(5a1) Go R & follow path 250 mtrs to junction with stone track.

(5a2) Take green track ahead by markpost for 350 mtrs to crosstracks.

(5a3) Go R 275 mtrs to cross bridge & climb to junction with small paths.

(5a4) Go L 350 mtrs to T junction. Go L 250 mtrs past barred tracks R to Y junction.

(5a5) Go to para 13 but turn R, not L.
****

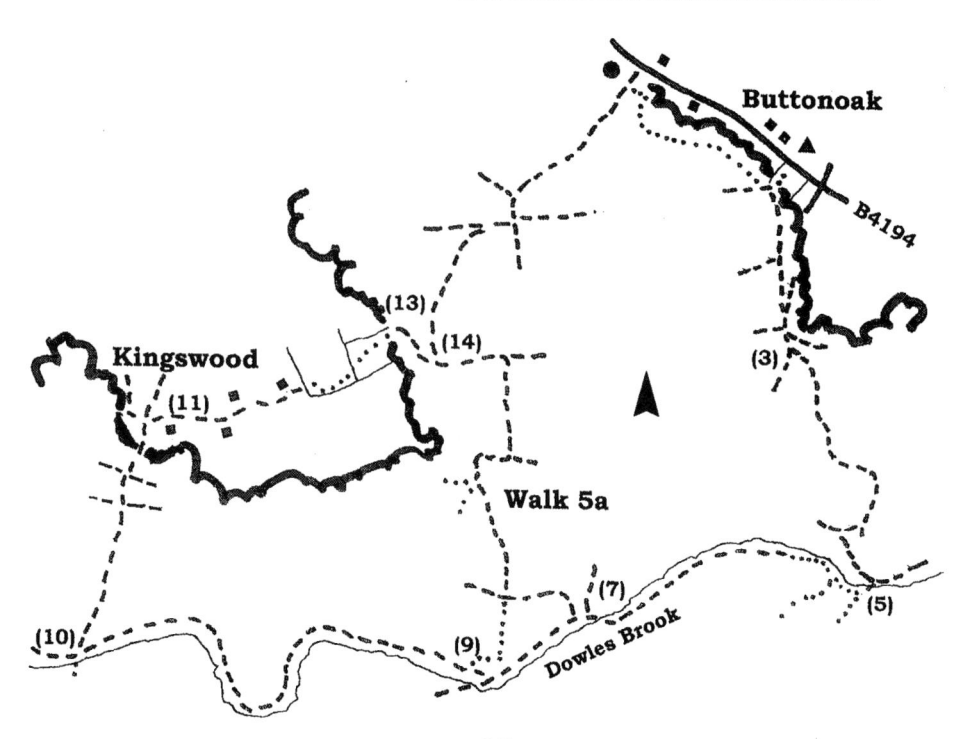

main Walk 5 continues
(9) Go ahead 2kms/1.25 miles (past 1st footbridge L) to T junction with footbridge L. (May be concealed by bushes.)

****
OPTION
To join Walk 4 turn to Walk 4 para 22.
****

(10) Go R 800 mtrs/.5 mile (cross stone track & earth track) & pass pole barrier to bend of stone track.

****
OPTION
To join Walk 11 turn L & go Walk 11 para 13 from "...follow...".
****

(11) Go R 450 mtrs to junction. Bear L past farm gate, follow green track to gate & cross stile into field.

(12) Go R, follow R hedge past ruin to field corner & cross stile. Follow hedged track & cross stile into field. Cross diagonally to bottom L corner, take small path & cross footbridge.

(13) Cross stile & follow hollow track 200 mtrs to junction.

(14) Go L 450 mtrs to fork. Go R to grass ride.

****
OPTION
To join Walk 9 turn to Walk 9 para 2 but turn L, not R.
****

(15) Go R up to stone track. Go L, take 1st track R & follow 600 mtrs/.4 mile to start.

Walk 9

Starting point: from the car park .4 mile west of the Button Oak pub
Length: - 5.5 miles/9 kms.
Walks you can join: Walks 11, 10 and 6.
Refreshments: the Button Oak.

Soon after the start you come to the broad grass ride which crosses the hill in a straight line. This has nothing to do with Alfred Watkins and his "Old Straight Track" but with the vision of the Birmingham Water Undertaking in the 1890s and the engineering skill of a Mr Mansergh. To learn more about the Elan Valley scheme see "The Waterworks". Later there are glorious views of the distant forest with a patchwork of brown and green fields, winding woodland paths and a cressy little brook. When you meet the open heathland of Pound Green Common you are near the end.

(1) From car park follow stone track 550 mtrs/.3 mile to junction. Go L to broad grass ride.

(2) Go R 700 mtrs/.4 mile down to near stone bridge, then bear R & cross timber footbridge.

(3) Enter field & follow R hedge 550 mtrs/.3 mile up to field corner, & take corner gate onto track.

****
OPTION
To join Walk 11 turn L & go to Walk 11 para (11) starting from "...follow...".
****

(4) Go ahead & take gate onto bend of stone track. Go ahead via gates till track ends at 1st field corner. Follow L hedge 500 mtrs/.3 mile to 2nd field corner, then go on 170 mtrs to pass midfield tree clump & take gateway L.

(5) Go R with hedge on your R 500 mtrs/.3 mile (past redundant stile) to field corner, & cross concealed stile.

(6) Go ahead & cross 2 stiles. Bear R to far corner of 2nd paddock & cross stile. Bear L through conifers & cross stile into field.

(7) Go ahead bearing R to middle of conifers, & cross stile into garden. Go ahead to pond, turn L past power pole, enter tunnel through shrubs & cross stile onto B4199.

(8) Care. Cross here, go R 80 mtrs to pass gate of Button Bridge House & cross stile L. Follow L hedge (via stile) & cross stile onto track.

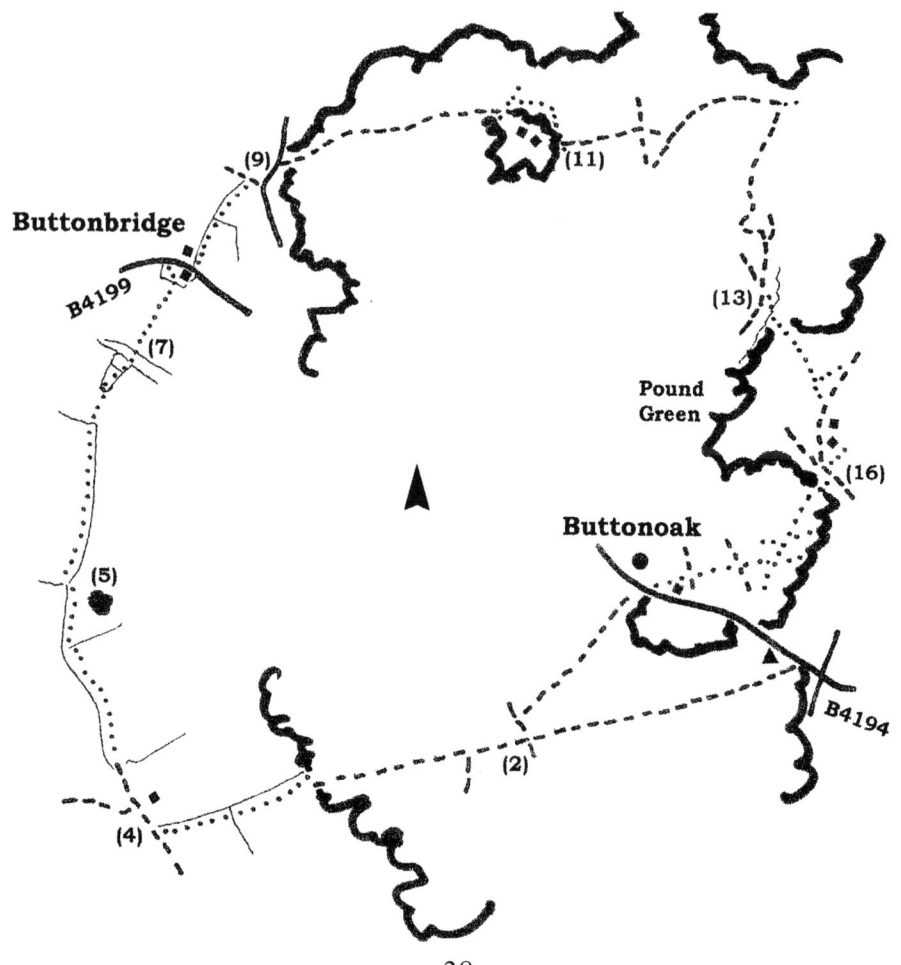

****
OPTION
To join Walk 10 go L 350 mtrs to R bend & cross stile ahead. Turn to Walk 10 para 12.
****

(9) Go R to lane. Go L 100 mtrs & take tarmac drive R. Go 850 mtrs/.5 mile to holiday park gate & cross planks L.

(10) Take R of 2 paths to junction. Go R & cross planks. Go 7 paces, turn L up hollow path & go on to earth track.

(11) Go L 300 mtrs (ignore faint forks R & L), cross wide track & go on 100 mtrs to stone track.

(12) Go L 850 mtrs/.5 mile round wide curve to pass stone track L. Go on 200 mtrs to end of earth track from R. Go on 30 paces & take 2nd small path L.

(13) Cross stile then plank, follow woodland path (past small path R) & climb to path junction with markpost.

(14) Go ahead (not L) to cross short plank, then bend R & follow timber fence to stone track. Go ahead on small path to track. Go R up to front corner of stone shed.

(15) Go ahead 20 paces to faint green track. Follow it R to stone track. Go L to gate of Cherry Trees.
****
OPTION
To join Walk 6 continue on track 100 mtrs to "Mickleford" & take path L. Turn to Walk 6 para 16 starting from "...300 mtrs...".
****

(16) Go on 10 paces, turn R to cross plank & stile into wood. Follow path to 2nd crosspath with markpost. Go R 450 mtr (over stone, earth, green track & 3 stiles, to B4199.

(17) Cross here & go R on verge to start.

39

Upper Arley
(Walks 6-6a, 7-7a, 8-8a, and 10)

This little waterside settlement with the forest for timber and the river for fish must have been a human settlement for millennia. On the east bank is the church, a cafe, a post office and grand Arley House with its arboretum. On the west side is a pub and many people's favourite railway station. The oldest structure is the sandstone church of St Peter. It was Victorianised in a restoration of 1885 but the nave and tower date from 1135 and other parts from the 14th and 15th centuries.

The lower reaches of the Severn were a transport artery from the earliest times, but for a period from 1727 the river was navigable upstream to Welshpool and Arley became a little port. Now it is a quiet cluster of brick, stone and timber framed houses around the quay and overlooking the majestic sweep of the river.

Arley Arboretum was first planted in 1828, making it one of the oldest in Britain. Low lying, sheltered and facing west across the River Severn, it has an ideal micro climate for rare and tender trees and shrubs. Go and see the Crimean pines, one of them is the tallest in the Briish isles at 140 feet high with a girth of over 12 feet. The branches of these strange looking trees grow vertically, parallel with the trunk. There is also a beech tree which has spread to cover a quarter of an acre. Branches have repeatedly rooted themselves so that it is not possible to find the original trunk. The arboretum is open to the public between 1st April and 31st October. Phone 01299 861368 for details.

Arley Station on the Severn Valley Railway has been restored in the style of the Great Western between the two World Wars. It has won awards for Best Kept Station and been used as a film set. For more see "Steam in the Woods".

From the 13th century until 1971 a **ferry** docked at the slipways on either bank until the last ferryman retired. It was replaced by the efficient but charmless tubular steel footbridge, a scenic disaster.

Walk 6 and 6a

Starting point: both walks start from the village end of Arley footbridge (east bank).
Length: Walk 6 miles/10 kms, 6a 4.25 miles/7 kms.
Walks you can join: Walks 1, 5 and 9.
Refreshments: a café and a pub at Arley, a pub at Buttonoak.

The first few miles follow the river, then comes a rise through the pine and spruce to 90 metres. Forest tracks cross a level plateau but then fall sharply to the Dowles Brook at 54 metres. This profile is more or less repeated past Buttonoak and Pound Green, with the final descent to the Severn giving views of the Victoria Bridge.

The cast iron **Victoria Bridge** was built in 1861 and was then the greatest cast iron span in the world. Now it is a graceful complement to the fields and trees and the silver river. For more see "Steam in the Woods".

A mile or so from the start of the walk you enter **Seckley Wood,** hanging improbably to a valley side so steep that at one point in a distance of 200 metres it falls from a height of 90 metres to the river at 25 metres. Near the water most of the trees are alder and willow which higher up give way to oak and beech. Some of it clings to perilous slopes where the roots must break up the sandstone rock to find living space. Walk 6a returns through the wood at a much higher level through mainly planted beech.

The little timber **chalet** sits on the edge of a deep, wooded valley. It is obviously inhabited by a gnome who wears a red tunic and red hat with a yellow bobble. Mug of spruce beer in hand, he smiles glassily over the treetops from his sunlit balcony, over the oaks in the foreground into the blue haze of distant conifers.

Pound Green is an open area of heather and bracken which was recorded in the Domesday Book of 1086. See "Special Places".

(1) From Arley village cross bridge to end of its parapet railings, then turn sharp R. Go under bridge & cross stile.

(2) Follow riverbank path for 3 kms/1.8 miles (under railway bridge & past gabled cottage) finally passing brick house to next stile on wood edge.

****
OPTION
To join Walk 1 cross the stile, then turn to Walk 1 and follow the river, as in para 27.
****

(3) Go up R 150 mtrs to meet stone track. Go L past timber houses to grass ride & brick water thingy.

(4) Go up ride 600 mtrs/.35 mile to next brick thingy by stone track.

****
OPTION
To continue Walk 6 go to para (5). **To finish Walk 6a** see below.

(6a1) Go R on stone track for 350 mtrs to crosstracks.

(6a2) Go ahead 35 paces then bear R on narrow, falling track. Go 750 mtrs/.5 mile down to gateway and stone track. Go ahead 400 mtrs to lane.

(6a3) Go R 750 mtrs/.5 mile to start.
****

main Walk 6 continues
(5) Go L 1 km/.6mile (past barrier and joining wide stone track) to B4199. **Don't cross here**.

(6) Go L on verge 100 mtrs then cross road to double gates & join earth track.

(7) Go 850 mtrs/.5 mile (ignore crosstrack & track L) & fall sharply into valley to meet track.

(8) Go R through steel gate plus 150 mtrs to stone track.

(9) Go up R 550 mtrs/.3 mile (round L bend & past 1st & 2nd tracks R) plus 30 paces, & take next (earth) track L.

(10) Go 400 mtrs to meet stone track.

(11) Go L 450 mtrs (down to cross stream & then up) to junction of tracks.

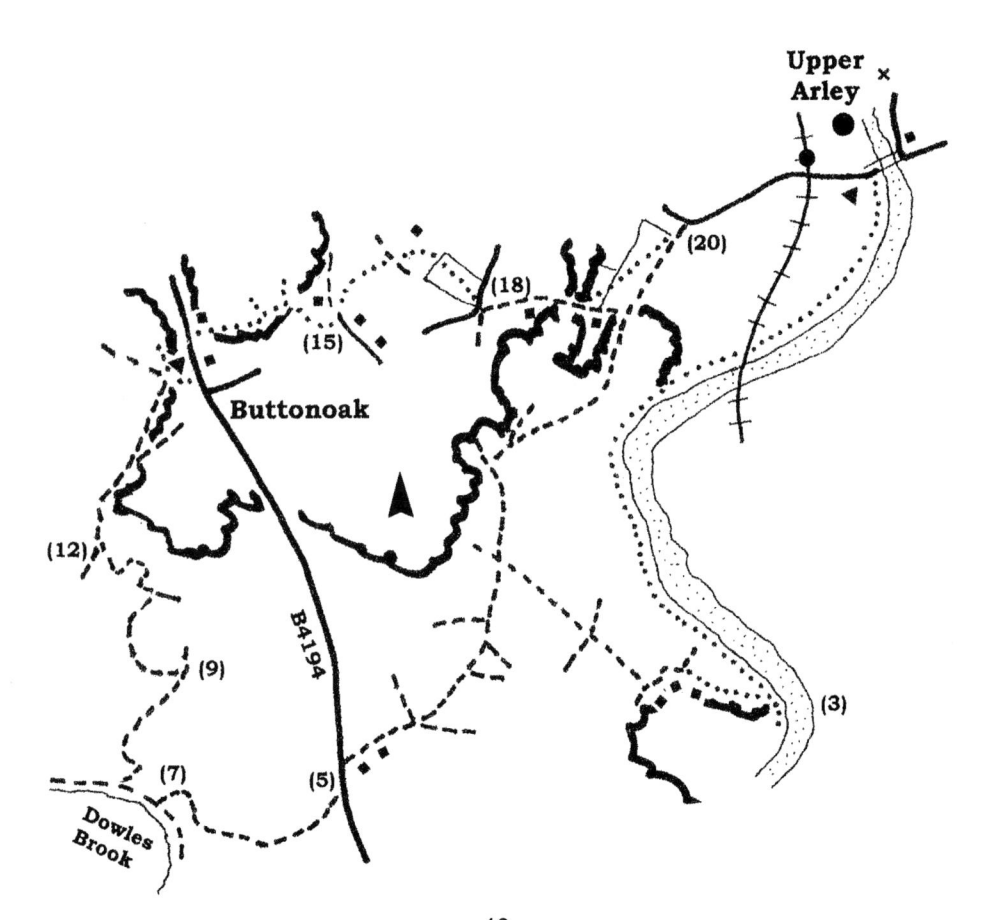

****
OPTION
To join Walk 5 go L 750 mtrs/.5 mile to junction & turn to Walk 5 para 4.
****

(12) Go R 500 mtrs (past track L & R fork) to wide grass ride, & take gateway R. Go ahead & take stile or gate onto B4194. **Don't cross here.**

(13) Go L on the footway 100 mtrs (past pub) to gate of 1st house L. Cross road into entrance opposite.

(14) Go 500 mtrs on hedged path, then along edge of wood to junction of grass paths by mark post.

(15) Go R to join drive & on to open green (Pound Green Common). Follow tarmac round to join stone track. Follow it to semi detached houses L (Mickleford).

****
OPTION
To join Walk 9 go ahead 100 mtrs to cross plank & stile L, then turn to Walk 9 para 16 sentence 2.
****

(16) Turn R on grass path 300 mtrs (joining stone track) to meet stone track by power pole with gizmo.

(17) Cross track & go ½ R across grass to cross stile in fence. Go ahead to midhedge gate & cross stile onto lane.

(18) Go R 20 paces & take track L. Go 400 mtrs to pass bungalow & sheds, & cross next stile L.

(19) Go ½ R (path is usually mown) to cross stile into poplar plantation. **Don't** follow field edge. Count 4 trees rows from L & take ride between 4th & 5th rows, down to stone track.

(20) Go L to lane. Go R 750 mtrs/.5 mile to start.

Upper Arley

Victoria Bridge

from Arley station

Walk 7 and 7a

Starting point: both walks start from the village end of Arley footbridge (east bank).
Length: Walk 7 – 6 miles/10 kms, 7a 5 miles/8 kms.
Walks you can join: Walk 2.
Refreshments: a café and a pub at Arley.

A gentle climb lifts you 84 metres out of the valley to mixed farming and woodland. The first wood is a witchtey tangle of close trees and brambles but the path has been picked out with yellow markers. The way through the much larger Eyemore Wood is wide and clear as you descend once more to the Severn.

Eyemore Wood is a long tongue of woodland reaching from the river up to Shatterford which was once part of the Wyre Forest. It has a great variety of trees. My hasty spotting showed oak, beech, ash, holly, sycamore, horse chestnut, hawthorn, Scots pine, larch, spruce and cypress, but I am sure there were more.

Through Eyemore Wood there are waymarks for The **North Worcestershire Path**, once a a 26 mile walk linking various country parks between Major's Green in Solihull and Kinver Edge. Until recently the Worcestershire Way lead from there and through this wood to the Severn then on to Bewdley. Now the WW has been cut short at Bewdley and the NWP extended to meet it. Odd .or what?

Victoria Bridge which carries the railway over the river is mentioned under Walk 6 and here you pass under it on the east bank. See "Steam in the Woods".

(1) From village end of footbridge take lane up & out. Stay on R side for 400 mtrs & take lane L. Go 300 mtrs, passing farm to drive R, & cross stile R into field.

(2) Go parallel with R fence curving up to top field corner & take gateway to drive. Go R 100 mtrs to near side of red house & take stile/gate L.

(3) Follow path to stile & field. Go R by trees 100 mtrs & cross stile R. Cross bridge & stile into field.

(4) Go ahead by line of trees to its end then bear R to projecting hedge corner. Go with hedge on your L to field corner & cross stile. Follow line of trees to power pole & cross stile into wood.

(5) Follow woodland path 175 mtrs to meet wide path. Go ahead 6 paces then turn L past oak & climb bank. Follow faint path (with yellow markers) & cross footbridge.

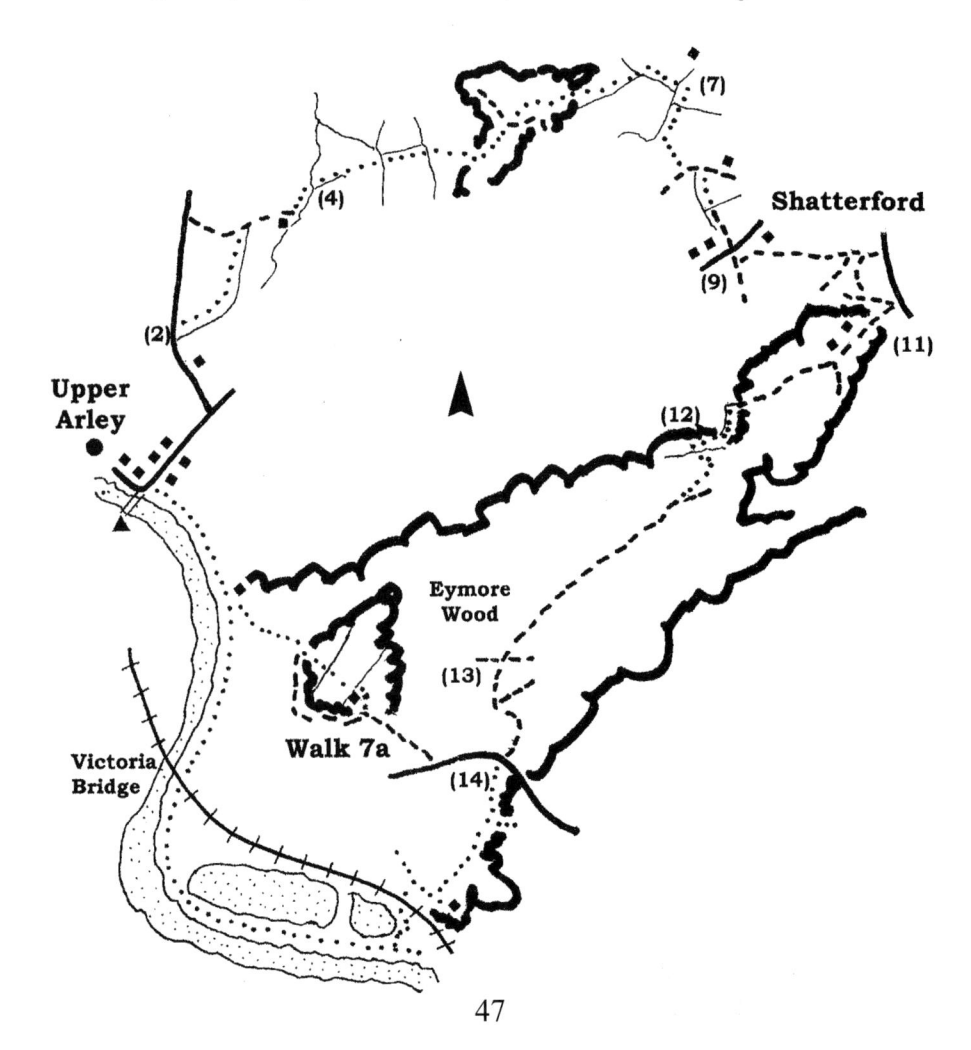

(6) Climb bank & follow path 120 mtrs to stile & field. Go ahead along R fence to field corner, & cross stile.

(7) Go R to double gates & cross stile. Go R by fence & cross twin stiles. Follow R hedge round inner field corner to projecting hedge corner.

(8) Turn ½ L to lone oak & join concrete track. Go L up to gates & cross stile R. Follow green track down field edge to gate & cross stile. Go ahead to drive & lane.

(9) Go R 30 mtrs & take track L. Go just a few paces & turn L. Follow track 400 mtrs to join a stone track.

(10) Go up 50 mtrs & take green track R to T junction. Go L up to T junction & take stone track R. Go 125 mtrs & take gate into wood.

(11) Go R on woodland track 600 mtrs/.35 mile & cross stile to fenced path. Go 225 mtrs & cross footbridge.

(12) Climb path & meet track. Go R 250 mtrs to crosstracks. Go ahead 650 mtrs/.4 mile to crosstracks.

(13) Go ahead on earth track to meet end of grassy ride. Go R on path & take steps up to car park.

****
To continue Walk 7 go to para (14). **To finish Walk 7a** see below.

(7a1) Turn R, go 250 mtrs & take steel gate R. Follow track 400 mtrs to wooden gates & cross stile R.

(7a2) Circle L round house & take small gate. Go ½ L via small gate to cross corner stile & meet track.

(7a3) Go down R to path junction. Go R to cross footbridge & follow riverside paths back to start.
****

main Walk 7 continues
(14) Go ahead past stile, cross road & take small path. Go 300 mtrs to gate & stile on wood edge. **Don't cross it.**

****
OPTION
To join Walk 2 cross stile & turn to Walk 2 para (7).
****

(15) Go R down woodland path 400 mtrs (past white gates & small path L) to meet main path. Go L down to gates & cross railway **(Great care)** to reservoirs.

(16) Go L around them to finger post near seat & turn L down to river. Go R on riverbank paths 2.5 kms/1.5 miles back to start.

Walk 8 and 8a
Starting point: both walks start from the village end of Arley footbridge (east bank).
Length: Walk 8 – 6 miles/10 kms, 8a 3.5 miles/6 kms.
Walks you can join: Walks 7 and 14.
Refreshments: a café and a pub at Arley.

Walk 8 starts with a saunter up one of the quietest reaches of the river but all the walks from places on the River Severn involve climbs. This one takes you from 30 to 130 metres in just under a mile (.6 km) but is very rewarding. Walk 8a is more gentle. Later there are wide views over the valley with the Clee Hills slumbering beyond. This is a quiet and genial landscape of small fields, big trees and thick hedges.

Nether Hollies is an isolated ruin with nothing standing but some low walls and a single corner. It was built in the local Triassic or New Red Sandstone seen in so many churches and farms in the area, but this is a particularly rich colour. Reached only by footpath, it is perched dramatically on the edge of a steep slope down to the river.

In the sloping, grassy field before you return to Arley there is a **pheasant** breeding enterprise. Some of the cocks are breathtaking, like my reluctant acquaintance dressed as a pantomime highwayman with black mask and gold and black costume.

****
OPTION
Walks 8 and **8a** finish together but start differently. Make your choice now.
****

Walk 8

(1) From village end of Arley footbridge go L past quay & turn L. Follow lane to car park & continue up riverbank 4.5 kms/2.7 miles. **Watch for:**
　　　　path becoming uneven & more wooded,
　　　　red stone house on far bank.
Cross wooden footbridge with railings then 2 plank bridges. Go ahead to double width stile but **don't cross**.

****
OPTION
To join Walk 14 turn to Walk 14 para (19).
****

(2) Turn R & follow general line of fence (you will have to circle round bushes) then when in view, head to pass R of stone ruin.

(3) Keep same fence on your L via gates to lane.

(4) Cross lane & stile then go ahead to projecting hedge corner. Go with hedge on your R & cross stile R. Go L by fence to field corner & cross stile.

(5) Go R by hedge/fence to pass farmhouse & cross stile R. Go ahead to drive then L up to lane.

(6) Go R 100 mtrs & take gate L. Follow R hedge to field corner & cross stile R. Follow green track 400 mtrs to lane.

(7) Go L 200 mtrs to 3rd house L & take gateway R. Go ahead on hedged track (if obstructed follow field edge) to join tree lined track. Keep this line via gates to lane.

(8) Go R 150 mtrs & take lane L. Go 300 mtrs to pass farm gate L plus 20 mtrs, & take wooded path L.

(9) Go 400 mtrs (ignore paths L) to junction.

****
OPTION
To join Walk 7 *go R* & turn to Walk 7 para (5), starting from "...6 paces...".
****

(10) Take waymarked path R. Go 200 mtrs to stile & field. Go ahead with trees close on your L & cross stile.

(11) Go ahead by L hedge & cross stile. Keep ahead to near end of tree line, then with trees on your L to field corner. Follow fence down to cross stile, bridge & stile.

(12) Go L 100 mtrs, cross stile L & follow path to drive. Go R 100 mtrs & take 2nd gateway L.

(13) Follow L hedge to bottom of field then curve R to R field corner & cross stile.

(14) Go L 300 mtrs to T junction. Go R 350 mtrs to start.

****
Walk 8a
(8a1) From village end of Arley footbridge follow lane past quay up to its end & take gates ahead.

(8a2) Follow drive & take gate, then follow tarmac track to iron gate & take gateway on its R. Follow L fence to cattle grid & bear L to cross stile.

angling at Arley

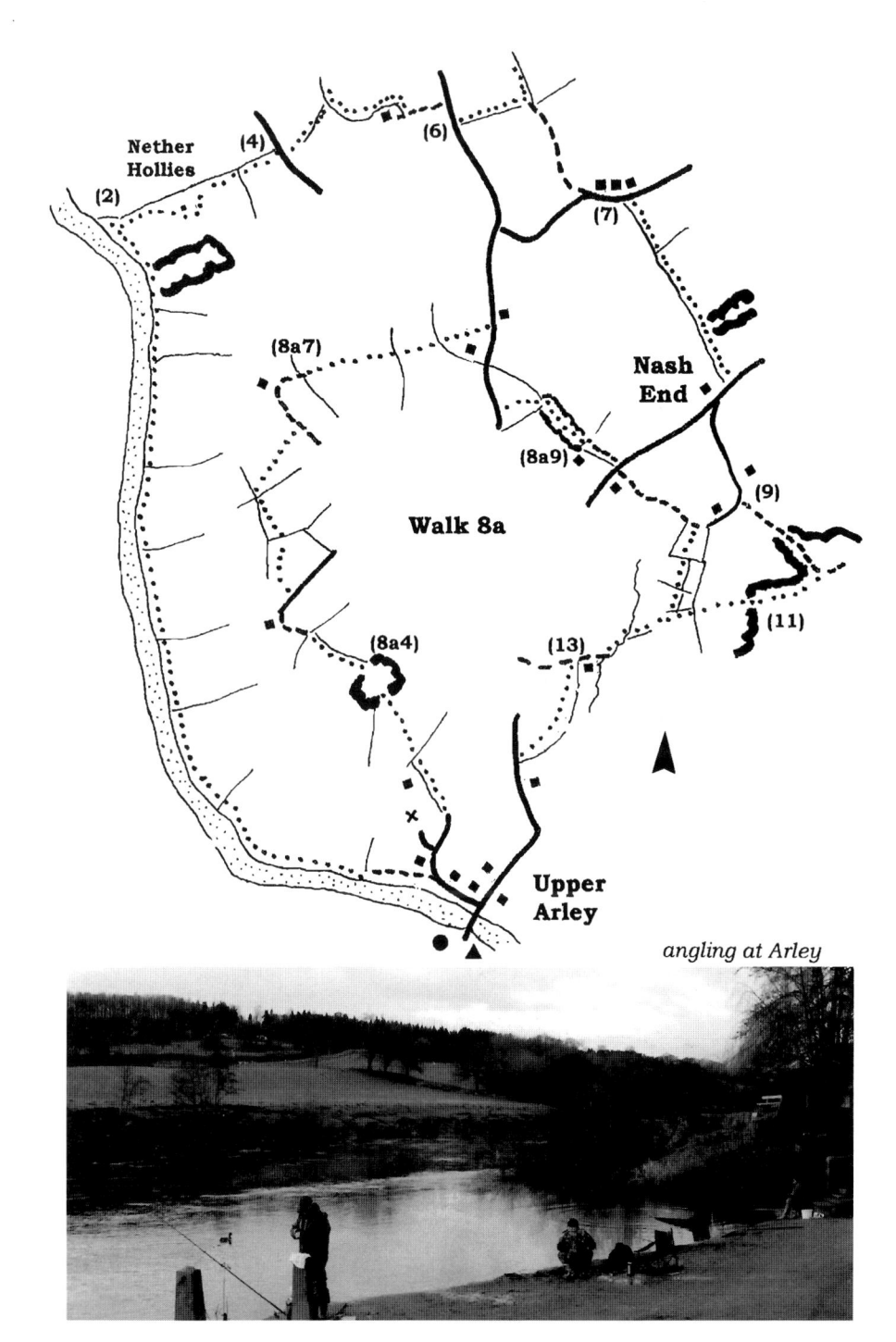

(8a3) Turn ½ R, head for nearest corner of wood & enter by big beech. Take path to corner of wire cage then turn L to pass big oak on your L & cross stile into field.

(8a4) Go ahead on track & pass farm to drive. Go R 50 mtrs & cross stile L.

(8a5) Bear R to pass midfield bush clump on your L & (when in view) follow remains of hedge down to cross stile. Follow L hedge & cross stile.

(8a6) Turn ½ R, climb bank & cross field to pass R end of woodland. Keep same line to gate & cross stile onto stone track. Go L, pass buildings & take double steel gates. Follow fenced track 75 mtrs to its end.

(8a7) Go ahead with fence on your R to field corner & take steel gate ahead. Head L of red & white house & take gateway into next field. Follow power lines to gate & road.

(8a8) Go R 300 mtrs (round L bend) to gate L & cross hurdle/stile. Bear R across field & cross stile.

(8a9) Go R on wooded track & cross stile. Follow R hedge to field corner & turn L to take gate. Follow track past farm to lane.

(8a10) Go R 50 mtrs & take track L. Pass farm plus 250 mtrs to handrail R, & cross stile. Go ahead & cross stile. Follow R hedge & cross stile.

(8a11) Bear R to near end of trees. Go with trees on your L to field corner then follow fence down to cross stile, bridge & stile.
next para (12)
****
Walk 9 is after Walk 5 under Buttonoak

*Nether Hollies
- Walk 14*

lazy summer river

*eastwards over
Ribbesford
- Walk 1*

Walk 10

Starting point: the village end of Arley bridge (east bank).
Length: - 6 miles/10 kms.
Walks you can join: Walks 9, 11 and 12.
Refreshments: There is the pub and the café at Arley but nothing else.

The first few miles is mainly through woodland with a steep rise from the valley (10 metres above sea level) followed by a gentler rise to the summit of the walk near Kinlet (134 metres). The return to the valley crosses high, open fields giving some wide views, but the best of it is the final tumbling descent to the Severn and the riverside walk back to the start.

There is only one striking sight on this walk, a huge, square 18th century mansion. It is very grand in small, red bricks with quoins, sills, lintels and a cornice of grey sandstone, but what a strange, isolated position.

(1) From Arley village cross bridge & turn R. Follow lane then earth track & take kissing gate.

(2) Face upriver, turn ½ L & head for railway signal. Cross stile before gate then cross railway & take stile.

(3) Go ahead & cross stile. Turn ½ R & cross stile onto track. Go a few paces towards farm & take rickety gate L. Go ahead up field to recessed corner of wood & cross stile L (not stile R with step) into field.

(4) Go up field edge with wood on you R, round R corner & go on to cross stile. Follow R fence 500 mtrs (.3 mile) & cross stile R. Go L to gate & cross stile onto track. Go ahead to lane.

(5) Go R 350 mtrs to Hungry Hill sign plus 25 paces, & take falling track L.

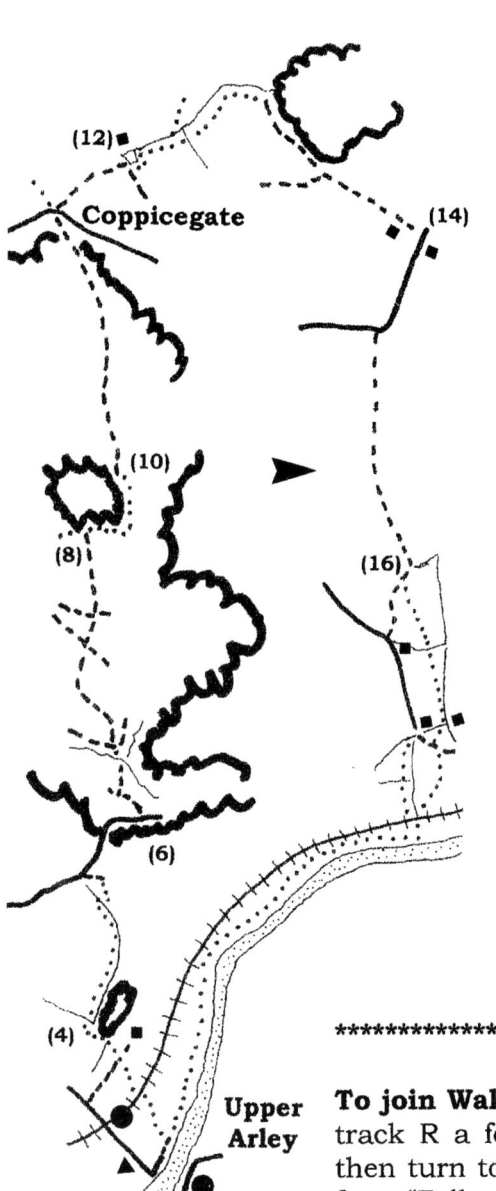

(6) Go to base of slope & take track R down to stream. Stay on L side till two steams meet, then cross onto rising track. Go L up to wide, stone track.

(7) Cross & take rising earth track opposite for 400 mtrs to crosstrack. Go R to stone track.

(8) Take track opposite for 400 mtrs (over crosstracks) to mark post by chalets.

(9) Take small path R to meet track. Go R & cross stream, plus 22 paces, then take small path L to tarmac drive.

(10) Go R 850 mtrs (.5 mile) to lane.

****
OPTION
To join Walk 11 go L to R bend, take track R a few paces & cross stile L, then turn to turn to Walk 11 para (6) from "Follow ...".
****

(11) Go L 100 mtrs to L bend & take track R. Go 350 mtrs to R bend & cross stile ahead.

56

(12) Follow L fence/hedge round house & along field edge, pass stile L & cross corner stile. Follow L hedge to corner of wood.
****
OPTION
To join Walk 12 take hedge gap L & turn to Walk 12 para (24).
****

(13) Go R with wood on your L to field corner. Take hedged, hollow track ahead for 350 mtrs & take gate into farm.

(14) Go ahead to gable end of stone barn. Turn R to join tarmac drive, go 370 mtrs to R bend & take earth track ahead.

(15) Go 800 mtrs/.5 mile (past tracks R & L) to R bend & cross corner stile.

(16) Bear L to far hedge & cross stile. Go parallel with L hedge & cross stile.

(17) Bear R & cross stile onto track, then 2nd stile into field. Head for bottom R field corner & cross stile.

(18) Go L under railway to river. Cross stile R & go 2 kms (1.2 miles) back to start.

Kinlet
(Walks 11 and 12)

Kinlet sits on a road junction in a area of level land surrounded by low, shapely hills As a village, in the sense of a cluster of buildings, the place seems negligible, but it is the centre of a large parish reaching from the River Severn west to the Baveney Brook and from the Borle Brook in the north to the Dowes Brook. It still has a school which draws children from a wide area, and its pub, the Eagle & Serpent. The name derives from the coat of arms of the Childe family who were the local squirearcy. The 13th century church sits strangely apart on a knoll in Kinlet Park

Walk 11

Starting point: from the pub.
Length: 7.5 miles/12.5 kms.
Walks you can join: Walks 10, 9 and 5.
Refreshments: the Eagle & Serpent at Kinlet.

In the first few miles we have a deep, woody dingle, a climb giving wide views and hedged tracks on the northern edge of the Wyre Forest. The return walk follows fairly remote and untrodden footpaths through a series of coppices and coverts on the eastern edge of the woodland. These were once connected as part of the ancient oak forest but are now separated and mainly under conifers.

(1) Face pub, go L 100 mtrs & take side road. Pass school & take stone track, then follow L hedge down to field corner.

(2) Take track into dingle, cross footbridge & take small gate.

(3) Bear R with trees on your R, follow small path through tunnel of trees & exit L onto field. Go up to R end of hillcrest wood & take hedge gap into field.

****

OPTION
To join Walk 10 *go ahead* & turn to Walk 10 para (13) starting from "...with wood..."
****

(4) Go R by hedge 500 mtrs (via stile & past stile R) to house. Circle L around it & cross stile onto track.

(5) Go ahead 300 mtrs to end of track where drive joins from R.

****
OPTION
To join Walk 9 go ahead to lane then turn to Walk 9 para (9) starting from "Go L 100 ..."
****

(6) Turn R, cross drive & take stile into field. Follow R hedge 350 mtrs (past stile R) to B4199.

(7) Don't Cross Here. Go R 100 mtrs to double power pole with gizmo. **Care.** Cross road & take stile. Follow path through bushes to lawn, go R & cross stile into field.

(8) Go ahead to gap in conifers & cross stile. Bear L, cross stile, follow L fence & take gate. Go ½ R & cross stile. Go ahead to cross stiles & track into corner of field.

(9) Follow L hedge 500 mtrs (past redundant stile) to field corner, & take wide gap L into next field.

(10) Follow R hedge 700 mtrs/.4 mile (via gate) & join stone track to pass farm.

(11) Pass track R & follow hedged track 150 mtrs (via gates) to field corner. Follow L hedge & take next gate. Go R by hedge 200 mtrs to field corner & cross stile.

(12) Follow hedged path then stone track 300 mtrs to junction of tracks.

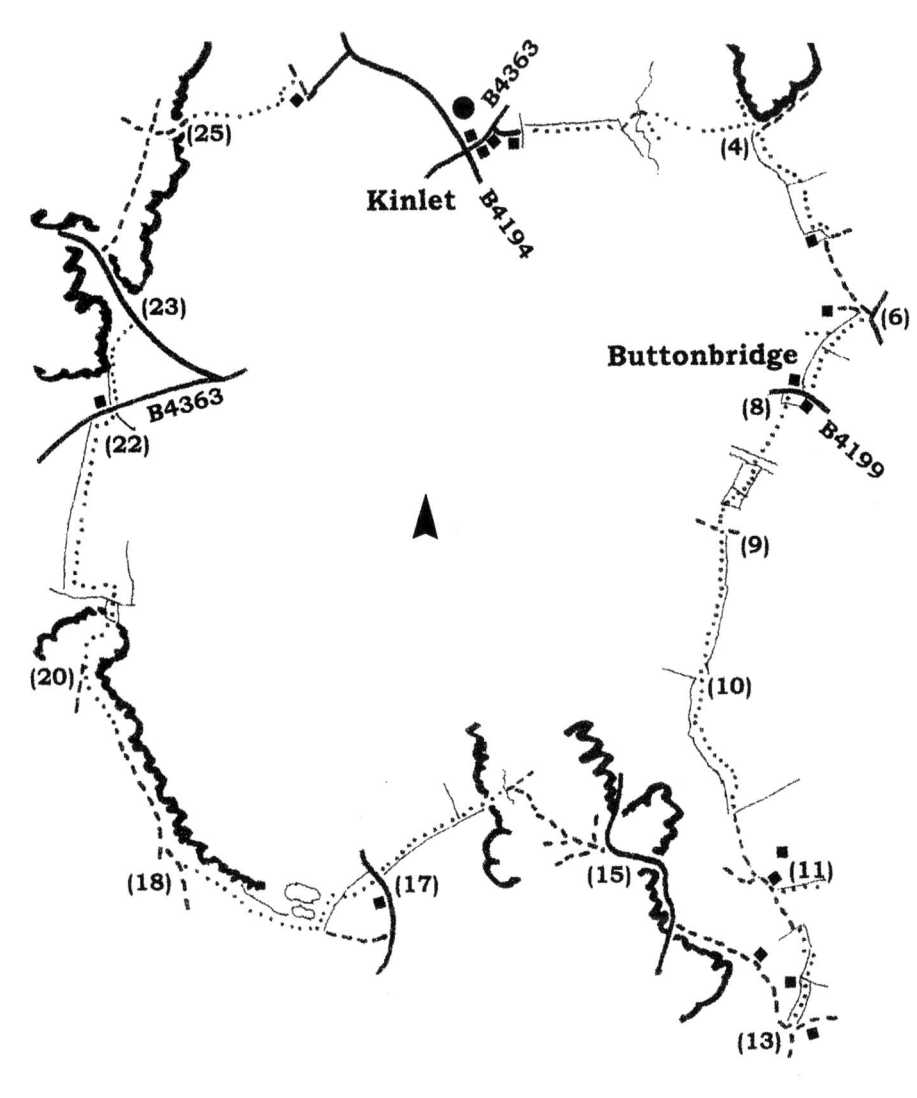

****
OPTION
To join Walk 5 *go L* & turn to Walk 5 para (11) starting from "...450 mtrs...".
****

(13) Turn R & follow stone track 600 mtrs/.36 mile to lane.

(14) Go R 450 mtrs (via L bend) to R bend, & take small gate ahead into wood.

(15) Go 75 mtrs to meet track. Follow it for 70 paces (past track R & ignoring green ride L) to fork, & go R. Follow 350 mtrs to junction & curve L.

(16) Go down, cross 2 streams, rise parallel with stream R past iron gate L to wood corner, & cross stile. Follow L hedge & cross stile, then follow L hedge to lane.

(17) Cross stile ahead, bear R & cross stile in R fence. Go L by fence to entrance track. Turn R, pass pond on you R & join path by fence along woodland edge.

(18) Go 400 mtrs to meet green track. Go R 100 mtrs to junction & turn R on rising green woodedge track.

(19) Go 450 mtrs to boggy patch. Cross & take rising hollow track for 200 mtrs to meet wide green track.

(20) Go R (over crosstrack) for 200 mtrs to mark post. Go R on green track, curving L to wood corner, & cross stile into field.

(21) Follow L fence & cross stile. Go L by fence to field corner, then R by fence 600 mtrs to gate. **Don't take it.** Go R by hedge & cross stile onto B4363.

(22) Don't cross here. Go R past house & drive then cross road & take stile. Follow L hedge then edge of wood for 200 mtrs till wood bears L at recessed area. Turn ½ R parallel with power lines & cross stile to road.

(23) Cross, go L 300 mtrs & take tarmac stub track R into wood.

(24) Follow woodland path/track 500 mtrs to 4 way junction. Go R 100 mtrs & take small gate to field.

(25) Go ½ R to further tree. **Look ahead, note power pole on summit** and head for the one beyond, to reach house. Go L around fenced area to track & go R to drive.

(26) Go L to T junction then R 600 mtrs to B4363. Cross & go L to start.

the packhorse bridge, Walks 12, 13 and 16

Dowles Brook at Far Forest - Walk 4

Walk 12

Starting point: from the pub.
Length: 10 miles/16 kms.
Walks you can join: Walks 16, 13 and 10.
Refreshments: the Eagle & Serpent at Kinlet

Woodland dominates the first part of this walk, with paths threading through a chain of woods and coverts spread over the hills on the western edge the Wyre area. The walk from there to the River Severn largely follows dense dingles along the Borle Brook, which I describe under "The River & the Streams". The level track followed on one section is the line of a mine railway and it now leads pleasantly to an old packhorse bridge and a new picnic site. There is more on the bridge under Walk 16. The best views are mainly in or over the Severn Valley, so that on the last, westward, leg of this walk it pays to keep turning round.

(1) From the pub, take the tarmac drive to Kinlet Hall for 600 mtrs/.36 mile & take stone track L.

(2) Go 200 mtrs & take track R 100 mtrs to power pole with gizmo. Go L up rough track to corner of land.

(3) IF there is clear path ahead, follow it.
 IF NOT go ahead to midfield oak, then ½ R & take small gate into wood.

(4) Follow woodland track 150 mtrs to crosstracks. Go R 700 mtrs/.4 mile (past 3 falling tracks R) to join stone track.

(5) Go ahead 100 mtrs to crosstracks. Go R 300 mtrs to edge of wood & take small gate into field.

(6) Go ½ L to join L fence. Follow it past gate L & take field corner gate. Follow L fence to gate & stone track.

(7) Go R 200 mtrs & take gate L. Follow woodland track 250 mtrs to wide earth track. Cross it & take rising path to small gate & field.

(8) Go R & take gate/stile. Follow R fence 400 mtrs down valley (via stile) & up to cross twin stiles.

(9) Head just R of summit to projecting tip of wood, & take middle of 3 gates. Cross field diagonally then (when in view) head 25 mtrs R of house & cross stile onto track.

(10) Cross stile opposite, go ahead & cross stile into wood. Descend steep slope & cross brook, then take rising hollow path & follow through wood to gate & paddock.

(11) Go ½ R to gate & exit onto stone track. Go R 350 mtrs to lane. Cross, go L 50 mtrs & take entrance R.

(12) Take path by R fence. Follow woodland track 250 mtrs (past falling track L) to wood corner, & cross stile into field. Go ahead to far hedge & cross stile 25 mtrs from L field corner.

(13) Go L down field edge, go round bottom corner plus 100 mtrs & cross stile. Go to bottom corner of field to cross bridge & stile. Go ½ R on faint path up to small steel gate.

****
OPTION
To join Walk 16 don't take gate. *Go L* & turn to Walk 16 para (12) starting from ".. through ..".
****

(14) Take small gate & go 550 mtrs/.3 mile to B 4363. **Care – don't cross here**. Go R 60 mtrs (past lane R) then cross road & enter track.

(15) Go 1.5 kms/1 mile to wooden rail R 25 mtrs short of packhorse bridge.

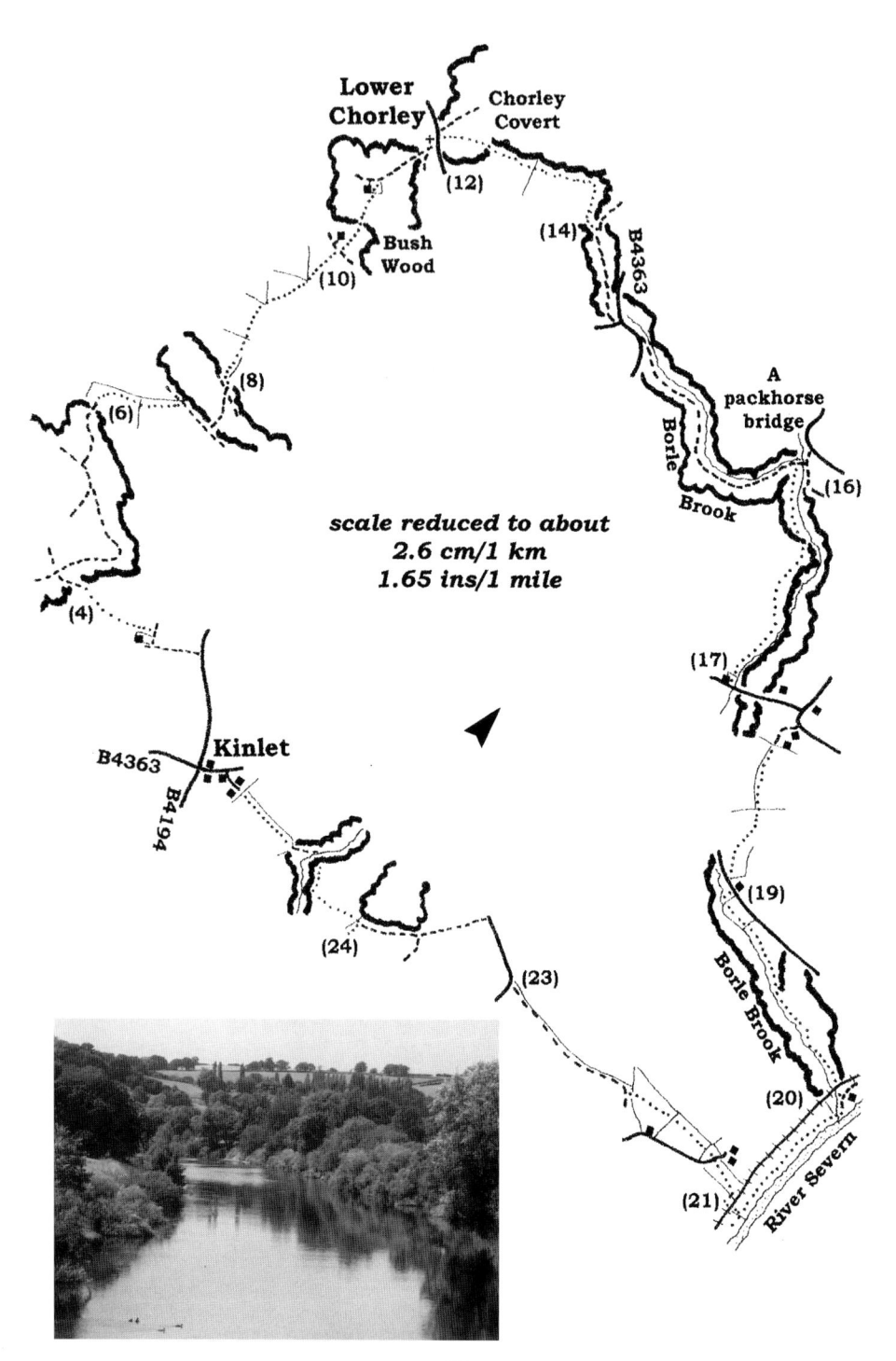

Lower Chorley
Chorley Covert
(12)
(14)
B4363
Bush Wood
(10)
(8)
(6)
A packhorse bridge
Borle Brook
(16)
scale reduced to about 2.6 cm/1 km 1.65 ins/1 mile
(4)
(17)
Kinlet
B4363
B4194
(19)
Borle Brook
(24)
(23)
(20)
(21)
River Severn

65

****
OPTION
To join Walk 13 cross bridge & turn to Walk 13 para (9).
****

(16) Follow woodland path 350 mtrs & cross stile into field. Follow bottom field edge 1 km/.6 mile (via 3 stiles & fenced path) to gate & lane.

(17) Go L 400 mtrs up steep slope to T junction. Go R 100 mtrs to L bend & take track R.

(18) Curve R past houses to end of track & cross stile. Follow R fence 450 mtrs (via stile) & take gate. Go ½ R down to take midfield gate, then ahead down to gates & cross stile onto B4555.

(19) Care. Cross road, go L 120 mtrs & cross stile R into field. Bear L down fence & take gate L. Follow R fence & cross stile. Follow line of brook R 1 km/.6 mile (via stiles) & pass under railway.

(20) Go ahead to brown gate & cross stile. Go ahead to river, turn R & cross footbridge. Go 800 mtrs/.5 mile to next stile.

****
OPTION
To join Walk 10 turn to Walk 10 para (18) and start from "Cross…".
****

(21) Go R to railway arch & cross stile. Go 35 paces & cross stile R. Go to top R field corner & cross stile onto track. Cross stile opposite, bear R & cross twin stiles into field.

(22) Go ahead parallel with R fence & cross twin stiles. Bear R & cross stile 25 mtrs R of big tree to reach earth track. Go R 1 km/.6 mile to tarmac drive.

(23) Go R to farm & up to corner of stone barn. Turn L, follow fenced track 400 mtrs, then grass track by wood 350 mtrs to wood corner, & take hedge gap into field.

(24) Go ahead bearing R & take gap into trees. Follow woodland path to field, then faint path to small gate & footbridge. Follow track into field & follow R fence back to start.

Alveley and Highley
(Severn Valley Country Park)
(Walks 13, 14 and 14a)

High on the west bank is the village of **Highley**. For centuries it was a farming community with some nearby stone quarries, but the terraced brick houses are unmistakably industrial age miners' cottages. The Coop store with its beehive plaque (1905) and the Working Men's Club tell the village's social history. So too does the grim, red brick Methodist Chapel, with its perpendicular style window ready to drop like a portcullis. The rest of the story can be seen by the river in the remains of the Alveley and Highley Mines.

The area around **St Mary's church** is much older. The chancel walls, the remains of three windows, a moulded doorway in the south wall and most of the nave are 12th century, or Norman. Alterations in the 15th century raised the height of the nave roof and added the present tower. More restoration was done in 1880. The timber framed house beside it was the vicarage until 1620.

Leaflets describe a History Trail and a Guided Tour which you should be able to get from the Visitor Centre in the Country Park.

Alveley, on the east bank, acquired its modern buildings much later. The oldest part of the village is on the crest of the ridge around the church of St Mary the Virgin and the Three Horse Shoes pub. There are rows of low, red sandstone houses but the oldest house is probably the timber framed Old Church House next to St Mary's. The extensive rest of Alveley is a pleasant but undistinguished housing estate.

The red sandstone church of **St Mary** was started in 1140 and displays more evidence of its Norman structure than many churches in the plain, sturdy pillars and rounded arches of the nave. The tower is also Norman except for the embattled top storey which was added in 1779. The chancel is rather later in a gothic style and the clerestory was added in the 16th century during the Tudor period. The interior is plain and rather dark because of the small, high windows. One early feature is a mediaeval wall painting in the side chapel. The east window has a fair sample of the stained glass of that famous Victorian, William Kempe, but what do you make of the strange little medallions in the otherwise plain west window? Go and look, and put lots of money in the box.

The **Country Park** was created on the site of the Highley and Alveley collieries which closed in 1969, with the addition of some surrounding farm land. Work to reclaim the unpromising waste tip and railway sidings was started in 1986, with grading, topsoiling, pond digging, tree planning and seeding. The result is one of the most spectacular and interesting nature reserve areas in the Midlands. The steeply sloping main site gives a panoramic view over the Severn Valley, the strange industrial legacy of both acid and alkaline soils supports an uncommon range of wild flowers ad butterflies. On the former farmland are wildflower meadows, pools and wetland. A small wood provides habitat for a different range of birds and flowers and contains a small natural amphitheatre used for drama and musical events.

Walk 13

Starting point: the Visitor Centre in the Country Park on the east bank, Alveley side.
Length: - 6 miles/10 kms.
Walks you can join: Walks 12 and 16.
Refreshments: there is a café at the Visitor Centre. Not far from the start is the riverside Ship Inn and near the end, at Woodhill, are the Malt Shovel and The Castle pubs.

The well wooded valleys of the Severn and the Borle Brook are lovely in all seasons, lush, leafy green or spidery black. I have said something about the course and water quality of both under "The River & the Streams" but on this walk you meet the Borle Brook as a secretive stream, flowing invisibly through tangled woodlands and thickets in its sinuous, private valley.

I particularly like the way the hills of the east bank sweep down to the Severn and the views from the higher points are glorious, from the summit of the grassy field on the first climb to the final descent back to the Severn.

(1) From Visitor Centre take drive from car park to 1st L bend & go R down stone track (cycle route 45) to cross bridge.

(2) Turn immediately L & follow riverbank 3 kms (1.8 miles). Pass Ship Inn to reach 2 red sandstone houses by railway viaduct, & cross stile in black fence between them.

****
OPTION
To join Walk 12 go back over the stile (sorry), follow river 800 mtrs/.5 mile to next a stile, then turn to Walk 12 para (21).
****

(3) Go R 50 mtrs to R bend & turn L under viaduct. Cross stile & follow brookside path 1 km/.6 mile. Watch for stile then boggy patch & take next gate, then turn R up to stile & B4555.

(4) Don't Cross Here. Go L 120 mtrs & pass house to entrance R. Cross road & take stile.

(5) Head uphill & take gate. Keep this line over the lower summit then bear R to top summit & take gate. Follow L fence 500 mtrs & cross stile onto farm track.

Highley

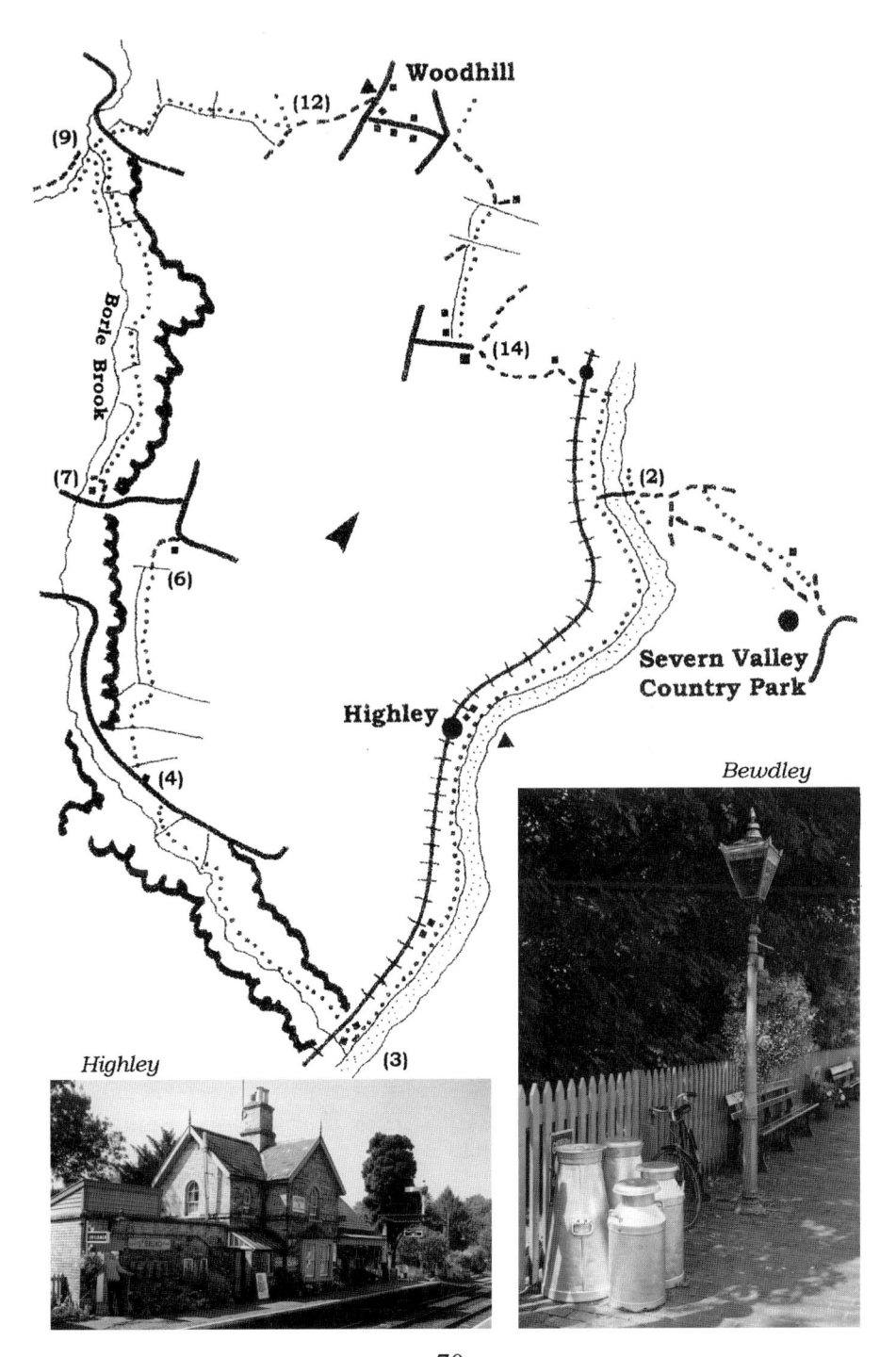

Bewdley

(6) Go ahead to lane. Go L 100 mtrs & take lane L. Go down 300 mtrs to 100 mtrs before bridge & take drive L by brick letter box.

(7) Go to L bend & cross stile ahead. Follow L hedge/fence 300 mtrs (via stiles) till fence bends L. Keep ahead on woodland path to gate, & cross stile.

(8) Follow R fence to gate & cross stile. Follow woodland path to cross 2 streams & reach picnic tables.

****
OPTION
To join Walk 16 go L down to bridge & turn to Walk 16 para 10, starting from "...,cross..."
****

(9) Take rising path to lane. Go L 5 paces, take rising path R & follow steps to stile & field.

(10) Go ahead across field corner, follow edge & cross stile L. Follow path to stile & field.

(11) Follow R hedge, cross stile & go through trees to reach corner of fence, then keep ahead & cross stile onto wooded track.

(12) Go L 350 mtrs to road.

(13) Go R to junction & cross road into Beech St. Follow past Oak St to junction & take earth track ahead.

(14) Go down 300 mtrs to L bend near farm & take recessed gate R. Follow R fence to field corner & take gate. Follow R hedge & cross stile onto lane.

(15) Go L to junction & take track R. Go 400 mtrs to meet three double & two small gates.

(16) Take small gate R & follow stone track down to cross railway. Go ahead to picnic tables then turn R 300 mtrs & cross bridge.

(17) Go ahead, pass track L & follow cycle route 45 back to start.

Walks 14 and 14a

Starting point: the Visitor Centre in the Country Park on the east bank, Alveley side.
Lengths: - Walk 14 – 6 miles/10 kms, 14a – 3.6 miles/6 kms.
Walks you can join: Walks 8 and 15.
Refreshments: there is a café at the Visitor Centre. In the old centre of Alveley there is the Three Horse Shoes and on the A442 as you start Walk 14 is the Royal Oak.

WARNING: Walk 14A is good in all seasons. Walk 14 proper follows a track, a half mile of which is liable to be rather overgrown by nettles and other summer vegetation. If you don't like that avoid this walk between mid July and mid September.

The walk climbs quickly from the Country Park and through Alveley to reach the other side of the ridge. There follows a long sunken track hedged by tall trees with occasional glimpses over an idyllic landscape. Crossing the ridge again you descend for a couple of miles through fields to the riverbank. A wooded stroll by the water leads you back to the start.

(1) From Visitor Centre follow car exit drive, pass hump warning sign to next bend & take either gate or stile. Follow path & take next gates. Fork L up to field corner & take recessed stile.

(2) Follow fenced path past 1st gate to field corner & take small gate onto path. Go ahead to road.

(3) Go R 150 mtrs to Methodist Church. Take stone path L to Oaklands then on hedged path to small gate & field.

(4) Follow L hedge to field corner with stile ahead & gate L.

****
OPTION
To continue Walk 14 go to para (5). **To finish Walk 14a** see below.

(14a1) Go R with hedge on your L to cross 2 stiles.

(14a2) Bear L to gable end of red O&Xs barn & cross stile. Follow fenced path & hedge to drive & road.

(14a3) Take gate opposite & follow L hedge through 2 fields up to stile. **Don't cross it**. Go R by hedge to gate & lane. **next para (15)**
****

(5) Take kissing gate L, bear R across field & take kissing gate. Go ½ R to field edge & take green track up to road.

(6) Cross, go L to railings & take fenced path to road. Go R 250 mtrs to A442.

(7) CARE. Go L a few paces, cross road & take footpath on R of vehicles. **If obstructed** go parallel with it to R end of black tank & cross twin stiles. Follow R hedge over 2 stiles to lane.

(8) Take green track ahead & go 2.2km/1.3 miles (farm R is about ½ way) to bend of lane.

(9) Go ahead 150 mtrs to T junction. Go up R (past lane L) to T junction.

(10) Go L 15 mtrs & cross stile R. **(If obstructed** see below.) Go ahead across field & (when in view) head for L side of wood & cross stile.

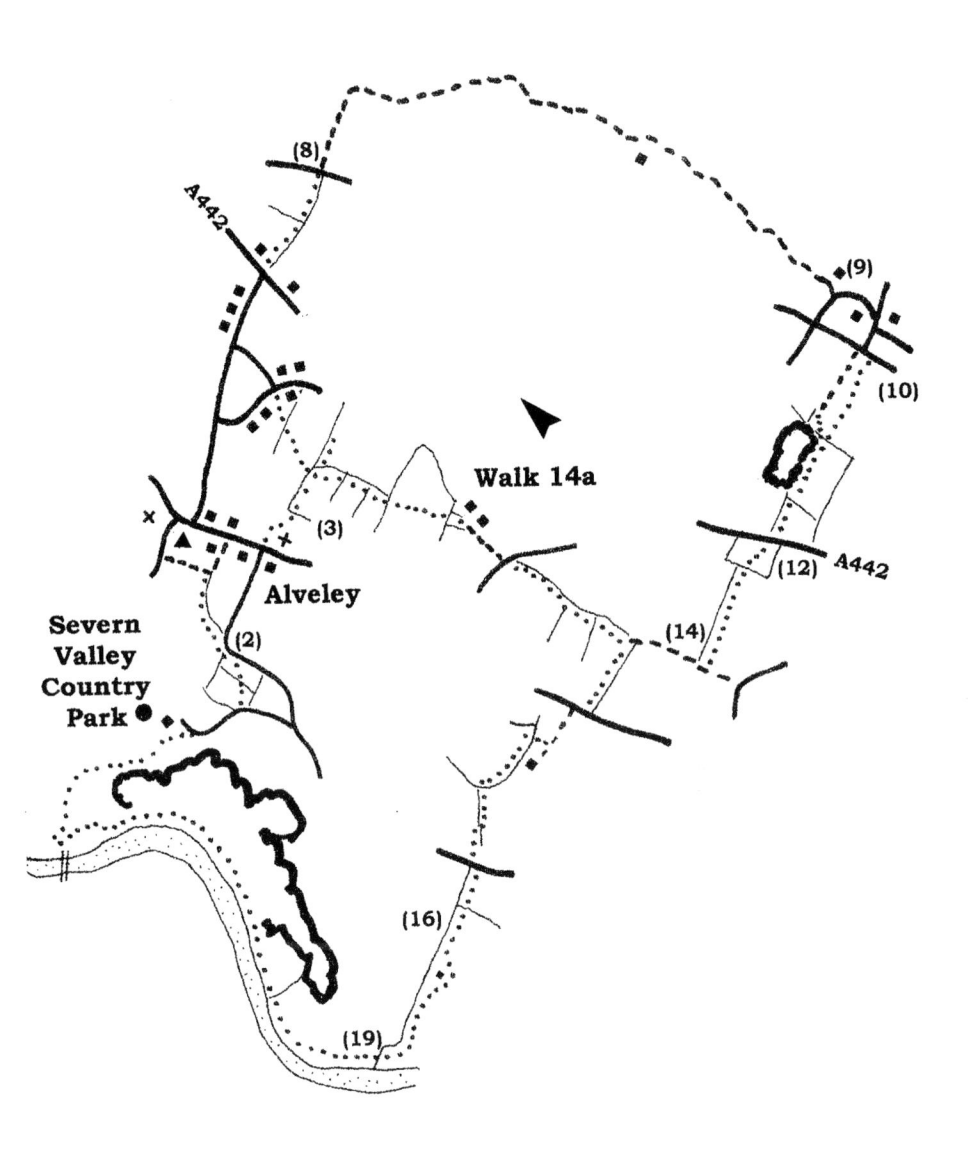

(**If obstructed** go back 50 mtrs & take double steel gates. Go ahead to ash tree then find your way to L end of wood & cross stile.)

(11) Follow R hedge & cross 2 stiles to A442. **CARE**. Go L 20 mtrs, cross road & take concealed stile.

(12) Cross field diagonally but cross twin stiles in L hedge 50 mtrs before corner.

(13) Follow R hedge to field corner & cross stile (if you can find it), or take gate onto track.

****
OPTION
To join Walk 8 go L 100 mtrs to lane & turn to Walk 8 para (7).
****

(14) Go R 250 mtrs to big oak then keep by L fence & cross stile into field. Go L by hedge & take gate onto lane.

(15) Go R 100 mtrs & turn L down farm track. Pass 2 barns R & disused stile then turn R to cross stile.

(16) Go L by fence down to field corner & cross stile L. Follow R hedge 100 mtrs & cross stile R. Go L by hedge to its corner, then keep ahead to stile & lane.

(17) Take gate opposite, follow R hedge/fence & take gate, then pass stone ruin close on your R.

(18) Go parallel with **R fence** down to river (diverting L round bushes) & find double width stile.

(19) Cross wide stile or normal one nearer river. Follow waterside paths 2km/1.25 miles to concrete bridge & get onto track.

****
OPTION
To join Walk 15 turn to Walk 15 para (12).
****

(20) Turn R & follow cycle route 45 up to start.

Walk 15

*steps to
Alveley church*

*ferry
Hampton Loade*

Hampton Loade
(Walks 15 and 16)

Where to start? Walk 15 is on the east bank and Walk 16 on the west. They are linked by a ferry which is open from April to September between 10.30 am and 6.00 pm. The west bank offers very limited parking, so if possible use the car park on the east bank (£1).

This small settlement is no more than a scatter of houses, chalets and mobile homes with the beautifully restored railway station the most distinguished feature. Even so, drowsing deep in the Severn Valley this is the ideal summer place to stroll, fish, eat and drink, or get wet and muddy in the low, slow river.

Walk 15

Starting point: the car park on the east bank of the river (£1).
Lengths: - 5 miles/8 kms.
Walks you can join: Walk 14.
Refreshments: the River & Rail pub is on the east bank, the Union Inn on the west. At Alveley you have the Three Horse Shoes and a café at the Country Park Visitor Centre.

This walk largely follows wandering, hedged tracks but the best feature is a beautiful lake in a dingle so deep and moist and fertile that it is almost buried in green plant life.

At a remote, high cross roads you will meet the **Butter Cross**, a red sandstone wheel cross of a Celtic type so worn that the cross carved into the circular head is almost flat. Butter crosses were places where country people would come to sell their produce but surely you would expect to find them in busy places. Most are in town centres, such as at Ludlow. Why erect one here? It is said that during the Black Death of 1349 food was left here for the plague affected villagers of Alveley, where 60% of the people had died.

Maybe so, but would the men, the cart and the horse have been available to carve, transport and erect it at a time of crippling labour shortage when a wooden marker would have done? And why, at that time, would they have carved a Celtic cross? Perhaps the cross was there long before the 14th century and the spot was just a convenient point.

(1) Leave car park & go R 60 mtrs to chains & ramp L. Go up ramp, circle R to R side of house then head for L side of wooden shed & cross stile.

(2) Take rising path into field then go with trees (later fence) on your R. Pass under power cables then head for L field corner & cross stile. Go R on field edge, cross stile & take path to meet track.

(3) Go R 16 paces, turn R on woodland path to meet track. Go ahead, cross footbridge & follow steep track 200 mtrs to concrete track. Go R 100 mtrs to junction.

(4) Go L 400 mtrs to pass 2nd house L & take track L. Go down to field corner & take small path ahead to meet track.

(5) Go R 250 mtrs to lane. Go R 100 mtrs & take track R.

(6) Go 200 mtrs to pass R fork then 300 mtrs to stream, & cross onto rising path.

(7) Go up 18 paces & take small path L. **(See note below.)** Cross stream, go 9 paces then cross again on gravel & take rising path ahead. Go on 200 mtrs to lane.

(If track is wet and muddy go from steam up to field & walk L round edge to lane.)

(8) Go L 400 mtrs to road junction at Alveley.

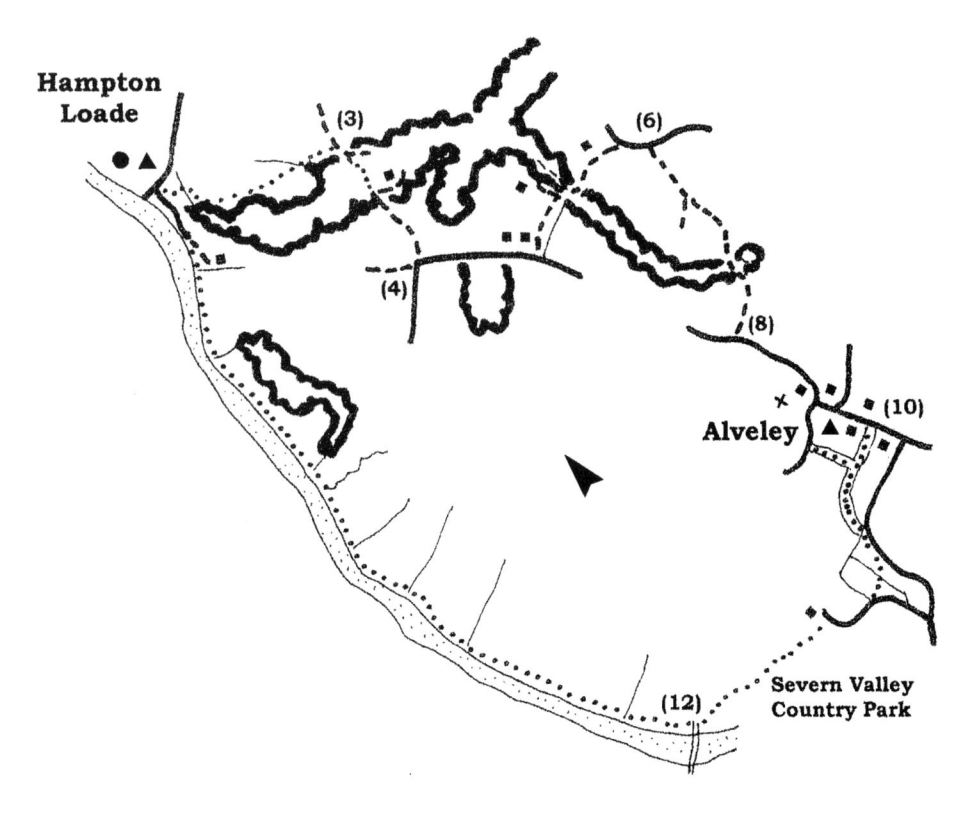

(9) Go L 200 mtrs to pass double steel mesh gates R then drive, & take path R.

****
OPTION
To join Walk 14 continue down street to Methodist Church & turn to Walk 14 para (3), 2nd sentence.
****

(10) Follow path 150 mtrs to corner & take kissing gate. Follow fenced path 300 mtrs, cross stile & enter field.

(11) Go ½ R & down to take double gates. Go ahead & take gates onto drive. Go ahead to R bend & take cycle route 45 down to start of bridge.

(12) Take path on either bank & walk **upstream** 3 kms/1.8 miles back to start.

(1) From ferry landing point walk upstream & cross stile. Turn L, pass L side of Unicorn Inn's patio, take ramped, walled path for 3 paces & climb steps L.

(2) Cross railway & go ahead through gate ("Private Land"). Follow path & cross stile into field. Go ahead & (when in view) head for R side of red bungalow to cross stile. Go ahead to reach lane.

(3) Go L to junction. Go ahead 250 mtrs to L bend & take track opposite.

(4) Follow 1 km/.6 mile & take small gate into field. Go ahead by R hedge 300 mtrs & take hedge gap onto track. Go on **only** 25 paces.

(5) Go R between hedges 100 mtrs to gate & cross stile. Follow L hedge 400 mtrs & cross stile onto drive. Go ahead to road.

(6) Cross lane L then cross main road & take stile. Follow L fence/hedge & cross stile. Go ahead through gateway towards next gate, but cross stile to its R.

(7) Turn L & go through trees to field. Go ½ R then (when in view) head for midhedge gate & cross stile. Go ½ L to projecting corner of mound & take small path across it. Follow field edge to stile. **Don't cross it.**

(Very Important Note: To visit the Malt Shovel or Castle pubs cross the stile & go L.)

****
OPTION
To join Walk 13 cross stile & turn to Walk 13 para 12
****

(8) Put your back to stile & go ahead to projecting hedge corner. Go with hedge on your L (through tree patch & gate) to bottom field corner, & cross stile.

(14) Cross road, go R & take side road. Go to R bend & enter drive of Cherry Tree House. Go to L of garage & cross stile. Follow fenced path to stile & field.

(15) Follow L fence & take gate. Go ahead with hedge on your L & take gate. Go ahead by midfield trees then keep same line 300 mtrs through gap in midhedge. Go on parallel with dingle L & take gate into wood.

(16) Follow path through wood & take gate. Go ahead by R fence to gate & cross stile onto lane.

(17) Go R 220 mtrs (over bridge to end of wood R) & take gate R to field.

(18) Follow R hedge to edge of cultivated area. Go on 36 paces to double trunked ash & take sloping path R. Duck under fallen tree & follow path down to cross brook at narrow point. Climb sloping path, turning L to stile & field.

(19) Go L & (when in view) head 75 mtrs L of red barn to cross twin stiles. (**If obstructed** follow hedge to barn & take gate.) Go R & cross stile

(20) Join track R, follow 200 mtrs & take gated track R. Follow to gate & field. Go L to 50 mtrs R of red bungalow & cross stile onto stone track.

(21) Go L 700 mtrs/.4 mile (past drive L) to B4555. **Care.** Don't cross here, go L to end of red shed, cross road & take stile.

(22) Follow L hedge to field corner & cross stile. Go on down L hedge, take small gate & go on to enter hedged track.

(23) Follow 400 mtrs & take small gate onto track. Go L 250 mtrs to lane. Go R down to start.

Walk 16

Starting point: ferry landing point on west bank.
Length: - 7.3 miles/12 kms.
Mud: The bridleway track in para 11 is likely to be muddy in wet weather. Take snorkel.
Walks you can join: Walks 13, 10 and 12.
Refreshments: the River & Rail pub is on the east bank of the Severn, the Union Inn on the west. At Woodhill there is the Malt Shovel and The Castle and at Billingsley the Cape of Good Hope.

Near the start of this walk you enter a long, green sunken track running just below the crest of a ridge which gives huge and verdant views over the Severn Valley. Later you cross an ancient packhorse bridge to follow a level track by Borle Brook.

The bridge was on the old road from Bridgnorth to Ludlow and here I met the designer and builders who had just fitted the new and splendid handrails. Elizabeth Turner works in Shrewsbury and designed the handsomely curved supports and stainless steel rails which are engraved with little pictures and historical information.

The brookside track that follows was once a mine railway and you can still see the remains of broken bridges and buildings. On my first visit in the early 1980s it was muddy and dismally shrouded in moist greenery. Now the surface has been hardened and some trees cut back to let in light.

For views this is one of the best walks in the book, with Brown and Titterstone Clee, Chelmarsh Reservoir and in the distant east, Wychbury Hill in the Clent Hills. Between are miles of hedges, fields, woods and hilltop churches.

Here and there you will see waymarks for the Jack Mytton Way, Mad Jack being an eccentric early 19th century squire and Shropshire MP. This 72 mile bridleway runs from Billingsley, which is on this walk, to Llanfair Waterdine on the Welsh border via Much Wenlock, Church Stretton and the Long Mynd.

*para (11) on Walk 16
- leave it till the Spring*

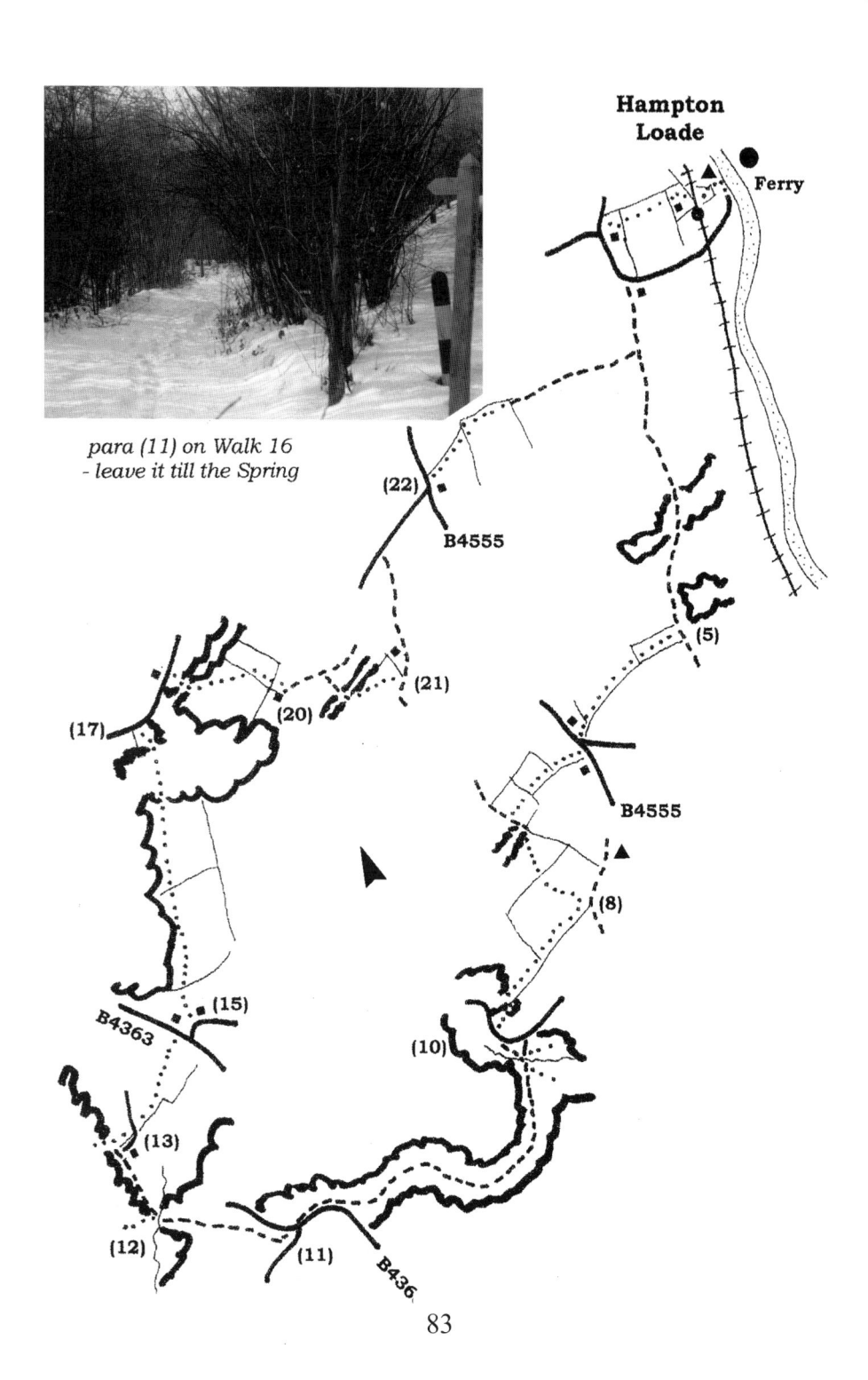

(9) Follow path (past steep path R) to stile & field. Go R & cross stile. Follow path down to lane.

****

OPTIONS
To join Walk 12 take stone track opposite & cross bridge. Go 25 mtrs then turn L & go to Walk 12 para (16)

****

(10) Take stone track opposite, cross bridge (pass path L) & follow 1.5 kms/1 mile to exit at B4363.

(11) Care. Cross here & go R. Pass lane L & take track L. Go 550 mtrs/.3 mile & take small gate.

(12) Go R through wood to open land. Go ahead with wood on your L & take small gate. Follow hedged path past house & take small gate into field.

(13) Go ahead by R hedge to field corner & take small gate onto drive. Cross & take small gate. Ignore track & follow R hedge 150 mtrs up to its corner. Bear L & (when in view) head for pub & cross stile onto B4363.

Old Red Sandstone on Walk 16

from Ribbesford Woods

looking over Upper Arley

beeches on Walk 4

Rocks and Contours

Our oldest rocks were laid down more than 2,500 million years ago but over the earliest layers were laid thick deposits of later material. The earth's crust is between 17 and 22 miles deep.

For eons the earth erupted in fire. Later, seas, lakes, tropical swamps, scorching deserts and frigid tundra formed and vanished as the land masses drifted together or apart and moved between the poles and the equator. Layers fell upon layers, deposits were crushed and compressed by those above. As continents collided the earth heaved or sank, folded and tilted as seas rose and fell.

The oldest rocks in the Wyre Forest and Severn Valley are in the Kinlet area. This crystalline, igneous rock called dolerite was formed deep in the earth some 700 million years ago from the cooling of molten magma. Depressingly grey, it outcrops in the Clee Hills where it is quarried for roadstone.

Our other surface rocks are sedimentary. The earliest were laid down some 400 million tears ago during a desert period in the Devonian era. They are called the Old Red Sandstone though they include clays and limestone. An area of these rocks runs northeast from just north of Bewdley to Trimpley and Shatterford.

During the Carboniferous era between 360 and 280 million years ago this whole area was a vast tropical swamp near the equator. Primitive, pine-like trees towered over 130 feet high, there were dense clumps of horsetails 50 feet high, giant fens and mosses. Enormous snails, crocodiles, eels and lizards wallowed in shallow lagoons. In the hot and humid air were dragon fly-like predators some 2 feet across, and on the ground were 6 feet long millipedes and 2 foot scorpions. Plants and creatures grew, died and sank into the swamp and over millions of years layers of dead vegetable and animal matter compressed to form the sedimentary rocks known as the Coal Measures.

West of the Severn from north of Bridgnorth the Upper (earlier) Coal Measures reach south in a narrowing wedge as far as Coppicegate. They are grey clays, sandstones, limestone and coals.

Running south from the western edge of Billingsley and encroaching over the first area is a widening belt of Middle Coal Measure rocks, with layers of grey shales, clays, fireclays, sandstones, ironstones and coals. These are the productive coal seams and the reason why there were mines at Alveley and Highly. These rocks reach south-east to meet the River Severn near Arley but south of this area both Upper and Middle types mix in a confusing swirl.

On the eastern bank of the river the underlying rocks are mainly Upper Coal measures as far south as Severn Lodge where they give way to the same confusing mixture as on the other bank.

Under Bewdley and running in narrow bands up both sides of the Severn is some Triassic sandstone. This soft, pebbly rock known as New Red Sandstone was formed from desert sand dunes some 230 millions years ago.

The contours of the landscape were largely created by a series of ice ages starting some 500,000 years ago and often interrupted by thousands of years of more temperate conditions. Repeated freezing, gouging and grinding by the implacably moving glaciers was followed by thawing and flooding, depositing uneven layers of ground up rocks, sand and pebbles. The last (or latest) ice in the Midlands started to thaw some 12,000 years ago.

In the later stages of this process our major rivers took to their present courses. The Severn was flowing north from Welshpool towards the estuary of the River Dee, but as more and more ice melted and dropped yet more rock and sand the outflow was blocked. Lakes formed and swelled and the water eventually forced a passage east to form the Ironbridge Gorge and then head south towards Bridgnorth.

Over the next 10,000 years the jagged contours of this shattered landscape were smoothed, sculpted and clothed by snow, rain, wind and plant life. And with constant changes in flow due to rain or melting ice, deposits of silt, collapses of banks and intermittent obstruction by fallen trees and debris, the course of the Severn shifted restlessly to and fro. This history is now marked by terraces on either bank showing past floodplain levels before the river cut down further to make a new channel. You can best see these former banks near Hampton Loade.

On the western side of the Severn two main streams flow across the forest to join it. The Borle Brook runs south-east from the Billingsley area and runs into the Severn just south of Highley railway station. The Dowles Brook runs east from the direction of Cleobury Mortimer. Both have many small tributaries. The ground shows a general pattern beneath this, and here I am painting with a broad brush, of two ridges running north - south, parallel with the Severn. The nearest to the river runs through high points of 130 to 170 metres between Chelmarsh and Callow Hill. The second, further west, has tops between 230 and 180 metres between Chorley and Rock. The result is a complicated landscape of small hills and deep, steep valleys.

On the eastern side of the river the landscape is simpler, taking the form of a ridge rising from the Severn in a single bank of fairly uniform height. The streams are fewer and smaller and they find their way to the Severn directly and independently.

This is not all of course, geology is the only thing more complicated than human nature. For a brilliant account of the geology along the railway get the leaflet "Explore Severn Valley Railway – Landscape and Geology Trail" at £1.95 from the Visitor Centre at Alveley and Tourist Information Centres.

The River and the Streams

The Afon Hafren, or River Severn when it reaches England, starts life as a remote pool on the high, bleak slopes of Pumlumon between Aberystwyth and Llanidloes.

The Severn gathers and grows in these wild, wet hills of Mid Wales, and its Welsh tributaries, Dulas, Clywedog, Carno, Rhiw and Fyrnwy, deliver sparkling clear water. The Environment Agency takes regular water samples from all our rivers and reports quality on an A to F scale. The Hafren/Severn is grade A as far downstream as the River Worfe, just north of Bridgnorth. From there to the Bristol Channel it is grade B; this is astonishing considering the poorer quality of some lower tributaries, such as the Stour. On its 180 mile journey to the sea many towns draw water from the Severn: Shrewsbury, Wolverhampton, Worcester, Coventry, Cheltenham and Gloucester.

Plants and Fish

The high quality of Severn water allows the river to support a wide range of fish. Between Bridgnorth and Bewdley there are barbell, roach, chub, dace, perch and pike. These are coarse fish which also flourish in the less pristine conditions of some other Midland rivers. More telling are the abundant stocks of salmon and brown trout.

Between wet and dry periods the Severn varies in level between 4.5m and 6m and it has cut an unusually deep and narrow channel for a lowland river. In winter the Severn races past, brown and bursting, and in low lying areas runs over the fields. In summer it murmurs genially round riffles of clean, grey stones and you have to clamber down high banks to water level. Low summer flows provide ideal conditions for the white flowering river crowfoot, water milfoil, perfoliate pondweed and fennel pondweed.

verdant Severnside

In flood the river lays down a thick layer of silt which acts as a fertiliser. This encourages docks, nettles and similar strong and common species but suppresses smaller, more interesting plants.

One feature of the Severn is the many eyots or small islands. They tend to have more varied and healthy vegetation because they are less directly affected by the surplus fertilisers which run off from arable fields. If you could reach them you might find chickweed, black mustard, Himalayan balsam, mudwort, almond willow, osier, tansy, slender tufted sedge and reed canary grass.

Down the River

Downstream from Bridgnorth the hills on either side of the river are quite smooth and rounded but high enough to make the valley very distinct. At Hampton Loade the ground rises from the river in gentle undulations reaching 100 metres in about a mile from the water. Here lanes run down to both banks of the Severn but there is no bridge. To cross the river you must use the ferry which swings across the river on a suspended cable. There is more on this under the walks from Arley.

There is no human settlement for the next couple of miles as the river banks grow higher and steeper. The valley bottom is deep between high ridges at the Severn Valley Country Park which was opened in 1992. There is more information in the Alveley walks.

From Stanley to Upper Arley there is little but fields and woods, the banks rising steep and green and cropped by sheep. About a mile to the south you meet the Borle Brook. This busy stream rises at Upton Cressett and curves south-east through The Down, Glazeley and a series of deep, dense dingles to join the Severn. In its 10 miles it is swelled by many small streams and two main tributaries, the Crunells Brook and the Horsford Brook. The main stream and all its tributaries are entirely rural and the water quality is grade A to within 1½ miles of the Severn, when it falls to grade B.

Riverside paths follow both banks with the railway to the west until it crosses the river by the famous cast iron Victoria Bridge. At Arley the road ends at the river and there was once a ferry, but it has gone and you must use the tubular steel footbridge. This is the start of the Wyre Forest, with Eyemore Wood reaching almost two miles along the ridge on the east bank. Most of the forest is on the west side and only reaches down to the river at Seckley Wood a mile downstream.

Beyond Victoria Bridge two sharp turns in the course of the river make room for Trimpley Reservoirs to be squeezed between rail and water. They supply Severn water to the local area of Worcestershire. Just downstream a mighty blue brick and steel aqueduct carries the Elan Valley supply to Birmingham. More of that under "The Waterworks".

From Folly Point river and railway straighten again and head for Bewdley. Woodland is never far from either bank although the east side is lined with chalets.

Just under a mile north of Bewdley the Dowles Brook joins the Severn from the west. It rises on the high ground of Wyre Common just north east of Cleobury Mortimer, then winds and meanders through the forest for six miles. Several tributaries join from north and south but only three are named on the map. The

Baveney Brook contributes its quota at some secret spot in the western block of the forest, the Mad Brook and Lem Brook join near Furnace Mill. The quality of the water is grade A throughout.

The brook marks the boundary between Shropshire and Worcestershire and in the past powered six water mills, a forge and a smithy. Furnace Mill is now a rather magnificent private house. Coopers Mill, south from Buttonoak is an outdoor and field studies centre for youth clubs. Knowles Mill about a quarter of a mile downstream from Coopers is preserved by the National Trust as a modest, comfortable private house in a pretty setting with the wheel house opposite. Town Mill, now a house, is a little nearer to the Severn on the other side of the brook.

Here the Severn Valley is still narrow but there are no longer ridges of hills on either bank. At Bewdley Thomas Telford's three arched bridge spans the river, the first in the 12 miles since Bridgnorth.

Bewdley was once a port which traded in all manner of goods; timber, wool, tobacco, charcoal, but the river is no longer navigable this far. Craft with more than minimal draught must stop at a shoal about a mile downstream at Blackstone Rock. The river frontage is picturesque on a summer's day but it often makes the news when heavy rains burst the Severn's banks and flood the town. In winter fogs, with ice swirling down the racing brown river, it can be a bleak place.

Bewdley, once a port

The Forest and the Trees

Worcestershire has woodland cover of about 6%, and this passes as well-wooded by our meagre British standards. In 1086 at least 25% of the county was wooded, and although that is more than four times the current level, it is only equivalent to the present density of woodland over much of Europe.

The hilly character and poor sandy soil of the Wyre explains why it remained forest in the middle of more fertile land. It is one of the largest areas of ancient woodland in lowland England; just after World War I it was one of the larger areas of all woodland. Of its present 6,000 acres almost half are still broadleaved trees.

In the Past

Long ago the Wyre Forest covered a large part of south Shropshire and Worcestershire. Royal hunting forests were established after the Norman conquest of 1066 and by 1300 they covered one third of England. In Worcestershire they included Ombersley, Feckenham, Malvern, and Horwell. These woodlands were owned by the Crown so all game, particularly deer and wild boar, were reserved for the king to hunt. This was not just a matter of sport but of food supply and revenue. The wild animals, the timber and the whole woodland habitat were subject to special and harsh laws. Death, mutilation or gaol were imposed for poaching, felling trees or even collecting fallen timber. As the mediaeval period drew to a close society, agriculture and trade changed, depredations into Royal forests were increasingly ignored and the harsh penalties were replaced by fines.

The Wyre Forest was held by the Mortimer family from the 11th century and was not a Royal forest until 1461 when the then head of the family became King Edward IV. Wyre was declared a Royal forest fairly late in their history and probably never suffered the full rigour of the forest law.

By the 1600s there had been severe inroads into both Wyre and Feckenham forests to supply fuel and charcoal for the north Worcestershire iron and Droitwich salt industries.

It was when the markets for coppice declined towards the end of the 19th century that many of the large trees we see today were planted. In Eymore and Chaddesley woods plantations of poplars are the remnants of a woodland market which never got off the ground. The trees were intended for matches but manufacturers started to import matchwood so they were allowed to grow on.

an oak at Buttonoak with six trunks due to coppicing fifty or so years ago - Walk 5

The Forest today

The Wyre Forest reaches from the west bank of the River Severn almost to Cleobury Mortimer and southwards towards Callow Hill, with Ribbesford Woods a narrow, riverside outlier to near Stourport on Severn. The northern edge of forest ends near Coppicegate. However the OS Landranger map shows many other small woods which are geographically and historically part of the old Wyre.

On the east bank there is Eymore Wood and to the north of it are Birch Wood, Coldridge Wood and Arley Wood. West of the Severn near Billingsley and Kinlet are Hook Coppice and Hook Plantation, Chorley Covert, Bush Wood, Gorsty Park and Birchen Park. All except the last have a good proportion of broadleaved trees.

The map also shows many long, sinuous belts of woodland on both sides of the Severn, the deep, steep, wooded dingles along the Shropshire brooks. They might have been coppiced in the past but now are usually luxuriant thickets. They have probably remained undisturbed natural woodland for longer than almost all woods, and may be surviving fragments of the ancient wildwood.

During the First World War Britain found itself desperately short of timber at a time when importing anything was hazardous. When it was over in 1919 the Forestry Commission was formed with a mission to secure the future supply of home grown timber.

The Forestry Commission have owned 2,800 acres of the Wyre since 1928, planting and harvesting a range of conifers with some oak and beech. The privately owned section to the west seems to be under a fairly coniferous regime but the Forest has still enough deciduous woodland, with its rich understorey of hawthorn, elder, blackthorn and hazel, to be a National Nature Reserve.

Since the 1930s, and in the absence of the coppicing which had been carried on for centuries, the woods have become more even aged and uniform. There is more about coppicing later, but it creates light areas with a ground cover which encourages many birds, small mammals and light loving plants. English Nature have set a target of restoring ten acres of coppice each year over the next thirty years, cutting poles for fencing stakes and firewood.

Oak is main species of deciduous tree in the Wyre Forest and both native varieties grow here. The Pedunculate or English Oak (Quercus robur) thrives in the damp alkaline soils of valley bottoms where limey deposits have been leached out from higher ground. Recognise it by its short leaf stems but long acorn stalks. Branches often form a series of dog legs creating a massive round dome about 60 feet high.

The Durmast or Sessile Oak (Quercus petraea) prefers drier more acid conditions on the valley sides and hilltops which tend to be sandy, gravely and well drained. Its leaf stalks are long but its acorn stalks short. The tree tends to be tall and straight.

By the River Severn at Arley there are magnificent hanging oak and beech woodlands on both banks in Eymore and Seckley Woods. Most of these forest oaks have several trunks, suggesting that at some time in the past they were coppiced.

About 600 acres of the conifers in Wyre are Douglas fir, originally planted in the 1920s. Others include European larch, Japanese larch, Norway spruce, western red cedar, Lawson's cypress and Scots pine. All were planted by the Forestry Commission, as were several hundred acres of beech.

The Forestry Commission's main purpose was to grow timber but over the years they have increasingly addressed non forestry issues. Most forests have been opened for public access, with visitor centres, nature trails and cycle tracks. There have long been sanctuary areas for deer, bats, badgers, grass snakes and other creatures. Planting schemes have put broadleaved trees on the edges of forest tracks, rides and along streamsides.

One feature of the early work was that the young trees were planted very close together. This causes dense shade which reduces weeds and lower branches get no light so they die and fall off, reducing the number of knots in the wood. The alternative would be hand chopping (brashing) which is expensive. Close planting has certain costs. One is that it encourages lanky trees with little girth that are vulnerable to wind throw.

Early Commission practice was to plant trees at intervals of 4 feet, or 1.2 metres. These days the distance is likely fall between 1.7 and 1.85 metres, depending on the likely future value of sawlogs. If girth is the aim it is best obtained by giving the trees space, balanced by the need to grow knot free timber.

In 1998 the Government published *A New Focus for England's Woodlands* which announced the biggest single shift in forestry policy since the Commission was formed. It listed many things that woodland could be used for, such as growing timber, reclaiming derelict industrial land, creating jobs, education, cutting pollution, recreation, enriching wildlife habitat, beautifying the countryside and improving urban and rural environments. Then it declared, in effect, that the new policy was for woodland to do all of these things. Timber growing is still an aim but must be pursued alongside the other aims in such a way that they do not get in each other's way.

The meaning of all this for the Wyre is that Forest Enterprise will in future manage their woodland less for timber than for amenity, and for the benefit of the plants and creatures, including two legged ones. For example, their Callow Hill centre has classrooms where rangers give talks, and the visitors include many school children working on projects. There is also a café with displays illustrating features of the forest. It is a good place to start a cycling expedition. Heading west on the A456 it is on the right 1 mile/.6 km after the water tower.

Special Trees & Special Places

The Mawley Oak
This great English oak still stands, after a fashion, at the western edge of the forest by the junction of the B4202 and A4117. For those who can use map references this is at SO 698756. It may have been left to mark a boundary. At head height the trunk is, or was, 23ft 6ins round, and though less than 90 ft tall its branches shade(d) more than a quarter of an acre. The large number of main branches suggest that perhaps 200 years ago it was pollarded. This is similar to coppicing, but the branches are cut off at a height beyond the reach of grazing animals. Quite recently the poor old thing has been blasted by the weather so that half the main trunk has split away from the rest and fallen forward. The standing half

seems to be alive but the balance of the tree has been destroyed and I suspect that in the next big storm the rest will keel over.

a huge, stocky old English oak in a small wood near Upper Arley on Walk 8a

The Seckley Beech dec'd.

On the edge of Seckley Wood to the east of Pound Green is a well (SO 762784). Within a few yards of the stream which flows towards the Severn stood a magnificent tree about 90 feet in girth. It looked like many trees growing from a single rootstock, and many people tried to count the trunks. Most lost count, but there were at least twenty six. Having survived for so long everything that nature could do to it, in 1990 the old beech fell in a storm. It takes with it the carved records of centuries of local affections and matches. Some of the hearts and initials were so old that they had grown way out of reach. Walk 6A passes the spot but there is not much to see.

The Whitty Pear

This famous tree was first recorded in 1678 when Alderman Edmund Pitts of Worcester wrote of the fruit:

> *"...in September so rough as to be ready to strangle one. But being then gathered, and kept till October they eat as well as any medlar".*

One source said the tree was of the species Sorbus pyriformis and was probably old in 1678. It survived until 1862 when it was burnt down by hooligans - vandalism is not as new as we like to think. Other reports described the tree as Sorbus domestica and there is a report of a field graft from the original forest tree in full bloom. Another descendent survives. Today, the tree expert, Alan Mitchell, calls the species True Service Tree, which is native to southern Europe and north Africa. It has green fruits and leaves rather like a rowan.

The Goodmoor Oak

stands at the junction of two lanes by the old railway (SO 723762), and very near the Betts Reserve, see below. It is a sessile oak with a single stem over 90 feet high containing about 13 tons of timber.

Pound Green Common

The Common tops a crest on the western side of the Severn Valley at a height of about 300 feet and a mile south-east of Arley. (SO 754789). Walk 6 passes through. It is within a sack like enclave in the trees open only to the north, and the boundary between Worcestershire and Shropshire runs down the west side. Depending on the season it may be a sea of waving green bracken or a wintry mixture of yellows, red, dying orange and dusky brown. Crowding round on two sides are the massed oaks and sage green conifers of the Forest, in this area mainly Scots pine, Norway spruce, Douglas fir and Larch.

This is one of the clearings in the Wyre which has not changed much since the Domesday survey. Historically commons belonged to the Lord of the Manor. The "commoners" were local people who had legal rights over them for limited purposes, such as pasture. Today commons are often owned by Parish Councils or local trusts but Pound Green Common is still privately owned. There are eight commoners whose rights derive from holding neighbouring land.

Verflors Wood

In 1989 The Woodland Trust were given two meadows covering 7 acres on the edge of the conifers at Pound Green Common. Walk 6 passes by. The site is level and the soil like the rest of the Wyre, but the land had been grazed for many years and nothing showed that at one time it had been part of the forest. The Trust have planted sessile oak in the central sections. Around them are faster growing but modestly sized trees including wild cherry and rowan, and shrub species such as hazel and hawthorn. The aim is to create a small broadleaved wood, the fast growing shrubs providing cover and protection until the bigger trees can look after themselves and to ensure that no one species will gallop all over the place and dominate.

Fred Dale Reserve

The reserve lies in the angle between the A4194 Bewdley - Bridgnorth road and the Dowles Brook at SO 772764. You meet it on walks 1 and 1B. It was named after Dr Fred Dale who left a legacy to buy a 99 year lease.

The Brook runs through the 57 acre site which is managed by the Worcestershire Nature Conservation Trust and the West Midland Bird Club. There is a mixture of habitats with a meadow managed for wild flowers and a scrub layer for such birds as the blackcap and garden warbler, an old railway embankment and cutting, woodland glades, a pool and the Dowles Brook.

In the water there are stoneloaches, bullheads, brown trout and crayfish. Nearby are kingfishers, dippers, grey and pied flycatcher, redstart, wood warbler and other birds.

Betts Reserve

This 6 acre Worcestershire Nature Conservation Trust reserve lies on the west side of a lane at SO 722764 near Furnace Mill. Park carefully on the verge and get in through a small gate on the north side of the cottages. You meet it on Walk 11.

The reserve lies on a steep, west facing slope down to the Lem Brook where there are damp areas. There is sessile oak, coppiced hazel, alder and ash. The acid soil supports wavy hair grass, bracken and heather, and in places dogs mercury and a small patch of lesser periwinkle. By the stream you may see dippers and grey wagtails.

Ribbesford Woods

On the west bank of the Severn south of Bewdley, these woods cling to a steep hillside and Walk 1 glances the northern edge.

From near river level at 30 metres the hillside climbs to 124 metres in 300 yards, and it is just as steep through the two mile long strip of woodland with an average width of about half a mile.

Although large blocks of the woods are under conifers the edges have been softened with broadleaves and the roads and rides are wide enough to let in the sun. This has encouraged flowers such as St John's Wort, common centaury, self heal, hedge woundwort, figwort, and birds foot trefoil. Butterflies abound, particularly meadow browns whose caterpillars feed on the grasses.

like a pantomime highwayman in gold, black and white - see Walk 7

Forest Plants & Creatures

Flowers, Ferns and Fungus

Walk west along the old railway line and along the Dowles Brook in early spring to see the sweet violet, marsh marigold, wild strawberry, lesser celandine and wood anemone.

These are common but the Wyre also has rarities, many discovered by the 19th century botanist, George Jorden, who visited the forest almost every day of his life.

Wintergreens are scarce everywhere but Wyre has all three British species - common, lesser and intermediate. Bloody cranesbill grows best in northern, alkaline soils and you would not expect to see it in the acidic Wyre Forest, but here it is on the Shropshire side of Dowles Brook. The brook and its tributaries cross several thin bands of limestone to pick up alkaline deposits.

Wild columbine grows alongside a number of the rides and paths in the Dowles Brook area and has been known as a wild plant in Worcestershire since 1787. It is just like the garden flower of the same name but is rarely pink or white and prefers alkaline soils.

Ramsons, enchanters' nightshade and lily of the valley are widespread in the forest. The lily is yet another plant of limestone soils but here it often grows alongside the acid loving bilberry. Greater and lesser periwinkles are pale, blue-flowered evergreen plants usually seen in gardens, the only British members of a family of tropical plants. Here they seem to be wild but might be garden escapers. The best places to look for them are around the old Wyre Forest railway station and in the Furnace Mill area. More typical of northern and upland areas are the mountain sedge and northern mountain melick.

George Jorden's 19th century visits show that Wyre was richer then than it is today. In a forest bog he reported that fragrant orchids were common but they have gone now. The bog was later drained and cut through by the railway but the area is still wet. Sedges and hemp agrimony grow there and the rare sword leaved helleborine is nearby. An old coal borehole is now a clear, deep pool filled with stoneworts.

In the Dowles valley there is some oak fern, a plant of cool, sheltered places in rocky woods and on scree. Although a poor competitor with vigorous plants it can tolerate heavy shade. Other forest plants include the tutsan, fragrant agrimony and sawwort.

In some parts of the forest less acidic soils were once planted as orchards. These are now neglected, leaving gnarled old apple, damson and plum trees. Remnants of meadow vegetation may survive beneath them, plants like harebell, yellow rattle, cowslip, green winged orchid and meadow saffron.

Beech trees are worth visiting in autumn when many species of the fungus genus Russula brighten up the ground beneath. In years when the mast ripens chaffinches are attracted to feed in large numbers and you may see a party of the closely related brambling.

In the Wyre hazel provides a home for the larvae of a longhorn beetle, Judolia cerambyciformis, which burrows into the old wood for at least a year before the beetles emerge. A springtime search of the ground around the bushes may also bring up toothwort, a delicate pinkish brown plant which is parasitic on the roots.

Rarely seen but found in wet and boggy places is the alder buckthorn. Together with the ordinary buckthorn, this is the foodplant of the brimstone butterfly larvae.

Creeper, Crawlers, Fliers and Fish

Wood ants are widespread in Britain but they favour certain woods where they live in their millions. You can't miss them in the Wyre. Rivers of ants may cross your path or your picnic and nearby you will find a two foot high structure like a tatty haystack.

The wood ant grows up to one third of an inch long. Each nest is a seething heap of activity with up to 100,000 occupants. You can get a painful nip from their jaws and disturbing a nest releases a strong smell. This is formic acid which the ants squirt at their prey and, in effect, pickle them, because the substance is related to the preservative fluid, formaldehyde. You may prefer to look at a wood ants' nest through a glass screen in the Forestry Commission's Visitor Centre.

wood ant's nest

A speciality of this forest is the **land caddis fly** (Enoicyla pusilla). The larvae of other caddis flies live only in water but this one makes its case of sand grains and feeds on dead oak leaves. They live in a small area of forest near the old Wyre Forest station. They had been recorded in 1879 were not seen again until 1957 when naturalist Norman Hickin camped in their patch. The larvae crawled into the tent and wandered onto his clothes. The adult caddis flies emerge very late in the year, in October or November, and the females are wingless.

More common but still very local are **glow worms** which are still found in the Furnace Mill area. Glow worms are beetles, the females produce a bright light but the males show only a faint greenish glow from the rear. The lights are produced by a simple chemical reaction.

Early **butterflies** include brimstone, small tortoiseshell, comma, orange tip and other "whites" including the small, large and green veined white.

Fritillary butterflies have wings of rich orange brown patterned with darker markings and the whole insect is quite large. Summer is the time to see the Wyre's two residents, the high brown and the silver washed. You may also see the dark green fritillary.

On shady paths on a sunny day you will see the speckled wood butterfly. Cream markings on dark brown make them vanish into the dappled woodland shade. They feed on woodland grasses and there are several broods a year, so the speckled wood is one of the first butterflies of spring and one of the last of autumn.

The brown family of butterflies includes the wall brown, meadow brown, gatekeeper and ringlet. The wall brown is quite common, the meadow brown more so and the commonest British butterfly. The gatekeeper is less common. Its caterpillars also feed on grasses but the adult butterflies like the tiny flowers of wood sage. The ringlet has a single brood in midsummer and is never common.

Hairstreaks are small, inconspicuous butterflies. The green hairstreak finds ideal conditions in the Wyre, feeding on bilberry, whilst the purple hairstreak lives on oak.

Moths of the Wyre include alder kitten, angle striped sallow, sword grass and red sword grass.

three views westwards

The Wyre has a wonderful variety of **birds**. In the coppiced oak woodlands with bracken, bilberry and heather beneath you will see, or hear, the wood warbler. More varied areas such as the Dowles Brook have more species of trees and also birds like garden warbler and blackcap. The stream itself attracts dippers, kingfishers and grey wagtail. Under the water are trout, chub, eel, lamprey, freshwater shrimp and crayfish.

The Wyre Forest includes many small open, grassy areas and old orchards which encourage species like redstart and pied flycatcher. Lack of natural nesting holes for these is due to the relatively young timber produced by coppicing and the have benefited from nestboxes.

Other birds of deciduous woodland like the Wyre: tawny owl, our three species of woodpecker, several tits, sparrowhawk, woodcock, crows, warblers and finches. In the conifers turtle doves, coal tits, goldcrests, redpoll, long eared owls, some siskins and crossbills breed.

Many of the mammals in the Wyre Forest can be found in other Midland woods but the **dormouse** seems to do best here. From *Alice in Wonderland* you will know that the dormouse is about the size of a house mouse but stouter with a bushy tail. They live for about four years and have an average of four young each year. Dormice eat nuts and fruit and the hazel nut shells they have eaten are quite distinctive. They gnaw a hole in the shell and use their tongue to remove the kernel. They are almost entirely nocturnal and hibernate in winter, for which offence one was unjustly placed in a teapot.

Dormice seem to be in general decline, though recent research into their habitat needs and putting out nest boxes has helped. They are mammals of coppiced woodland but they do not flourish where large blocks of trees are coppiced at the same time. They are tree dwellers and seldom come to the ground, so where large scale coppicing prevents them from moving around through the treetops, they decline.

Reptiles and amphibians are retiring species but you may see grass snakes and adders. The grass snake is usually longer and more likely to be found in damp places, often swimming in ponds and streams where it may catch newts and fish.

You can tell Britain's only poisonous snake, the adder, by a dark zigzag line down its back. They often lie out in sunny spots by the side of paths but they can feel ground vibrations of approaching walkers and slither out of sight. Adders only bite if handled or cornered so if you meet one just let it be. More people in Britain die from bee stings each year than were killed by adder bites in the last century.

The common lizard is also very retiring and will usually vanish long before you see it. Slow worms are often confused with snakes but they are lizards without legs. They are only twelve to eighteen inches long and generally light greyish brown. They eat insects and other invertebrates including small slugs and their young are born in late summer.

As the weather turns colder, slow worms, grass snakes, adders and common lizards hibernate, though they may come out to sun themselves on the occasional warm winter's day.

The Deer

Wyre Forest has great numbers of small creatures; wood ants, caddis fly, glow worms and dormice, but nothing gives people more pleasure than seeing large ones.

We have six species of deer in Britain but only three of them are native - red, fallow and roe, although the fallow deer were introduced by the Romans. Muntjac deer originate from India and China but have spread into most woodlands in southern and midland England. Two other introduced species live in restricted areas, sika deer from Japan and Chinese water deer. In the Wyre we have just fallow, roe and muntjac.

Deer are browsers that eat tree shoots, grasses, fungi, acorns and chestnuts, brambles, gorse and heather. And if they find themselves in arable fields or gardens they are quite happy with cereals and root crops, peas, beans and carrots.

Deer can multiply rapidly and their numbers are limited by the amount of food available in the harsher winter months. Even so, in a mild winter the fallow deer in the Wyre can start to outgrow their food supply. At one time wolves controlled the population by picking off the weakest and so ensuring the survival and quality of the herd. But the last British wolf was killed about 300 years ago, and with no other natural predator control depends on the cruelty of starvation or human marksmen. A skilled ranger who can shoot selected quarry cleanly is by far the most humane control. Forest Enterprise try to keep the population of fallow deer (the largest group) at about 150 so that the food of the forest is sufficient and they will not roam onto adjacent land to interfere with farms or gardens.

Fallow deer now roam wild over the whole Wyre Forest. They were extinct here by the 16th century and the present population are descended from escapees from Mawley Park about 100 years ago.

Most fallow are chestnut brown with white spots in summer but they become greyer and less spotted in winter. There is also a pale version. Mixed with them will be the black variety, which are dusky brown in winter, and sometimes white fallow which vary in colour from sandy to cream. Fallow have long white tails with a thick black stripe.

Bucks grow to about a metre high at the shoulder and weigh 150 to 200 pounds. They grow "palmate" antlers, a long wing shape with spikes, very different from the red stag familiar from road signs, Victorian paintings, shortbread tins and whisky bottles.

Fallow bucks spend the summer alone or in a sort of rugby club with other bucks. As with the famous ball at Kirriemuir, the does join them from early October when the rut takes place on traditional rutting grounds. It lasts about four weeks but the fawns are not born until the next May or June.

Roe deer are found in small numbers all over the Wyre living singly or in family groups of a buck, a doe and kids. They are reddish brown in summer, pale brown to grey in winter. Roe are tailess but both sexes have a white patch on the rump, the buck's much larger. When they are alarmed the hairs erect to increase the size of the patch.

Bucks can reach a height of 80cm at the shoulder. The antlers are small and simple with short stems bearing three short tines and with advancing age small lumps called pearls appear on the stems. Look out for one of the many pubs named The Roebuck and you will get the idea.

The antlers are cast between November and January and will be fully grown again by April. From this time until August bucks become aggressive in defending their territory until the rut, which runs from mid July until the end of August. Fawns are born in May and June and will often be twins and sometimes triplets.

Muntjac deer were introduced into Woburn Park, Bedfordshire during the 19th century but, being no bigger than a dog, they soon slipped out into the fields and hedgerows to spread across the county. Gradually they colonised most woodlands in the south and midlands and were first seen in the Wyre in the early 1960s. You will be lucky to see them because they rarely grow bigger than 70 cm at the shoulder and can hide in bracken or brambles.

They are red-brown in colour and seem rather hunch backed. The bucks' antlers reach only about 10 cm. Muntjac live in small, family groups and can breed all the year round.

I have certainly seen fallow deer in the Wyre but never so many as I have met on Cannock Chase or, strangely, in the hilly arable land of south Warwickshire. Roe I have met only twice. Muntjac I have seen in many woods and gardens though never in the Wyre.

Be watchful, tread softly and good luck, but here are two warnings. (1) **Never** touch a lone fawn. It has not been abandoned but it will be if you interfere. (2) **Drive carefully** by day or night. Deer can break out yards in front of your car and each year many are killed by traffic. And think of the dent.

Charcoal, Bark & Coal

Timbers for such buildings as Ribbesford Church and the Bailiff's House in Bewdley came from the comparatively few standard trees in the Wyre Forest because for many centuries most of the trees had been coppiced

Coppicing

If you cut back young broadleaved trees the stumps will shoot and grow a mass of small stems. After 15 years or so they can be harvested, and again 15 years later. Coppicing gave fuel for charcoal burning and salt evaporation, palings, stakes, peasticks, baskets, hurdles and firewood.

Coppicing was managed by dividing the wood into areas called "falls" and modern maps show the names of many: Oxbind Coppice, Bells Coppice, Gibbonswell Coppice etc. They were cut on a rotation of between 14 and 20 years, and for the first 5 or 7 years would be enclosed to protect the regrowth from browsing animals.

In Worcestershire there was great demand from the hopyards for ash poles, so ash beds were common in the Wyre. The trees were planted four feet apart with four poles per stool, and the beds could grow up to 10,000 poles per acre. As an alternative to ash they sometimes grew lime and larch. Hazel was widely coppiced for bean poles, basketry, wattle hurdles and thatching spars.

Although large scale coppicing died out after World War II some trees still show traces. They may have several main trunks starting from ground level, others have a single main stem which starts with a sideways bend where a side shoot grew from the stool. Sometimes enveloping occurs, when a new trunk completely covers the old stool to produce a "false standard". Fungi and disease will have attacked the stool so the tree will not give the timber it promises.

Charcoal for iron smelting was originally made on flat, circular hearths, shallow excavations in the forest floor about 10 feet in diameter. They are now long overgrown and returned to nature but some are still recognisable. Four foot poles were laid in a dense conical stack, a fire lit at the centre and the stack roofed with turves to exclude air. A big stack might take four or five days to burn up. They needed constant attention because the turf tended to dry and burn and had to be augmented and damped.

Later metal retorts were used, the sides formed by three circular units fitting one above the other and topped with a lid. They had the advantage that air was efficiently excluded without turves and the retort could be left alone to burn.

Given the choice, the charcoal burners preferred to use holly or beech. Oak produces a flakier charcoal, whilst ash, elm, birch and willow all make a charcoal which is less dense. The last large scale commercial charcoal production was during the Second World War opposite the Green Dragon at Fingerpost, the junction of the Ludlow and Leominster roads.

Tanning

Trees were also essential to the Bewdley tanning industry where the bark provided tannin for the leather. Bark can only be stripped from oaks when the sap is rising and the leaves bursting from the bud. Tradition in Bewdley had it that this was between 24th April and 14th June. Men cut the wood and trimmed the side shoots whilst women peeled the bark. The poles were placed on X or Y shaped supports and gangs of up to forty would peel using a special tool. Each tree took several hours. The peeled bark was laid inner side down to stop rain leaching out the tannic acid. The stripped poles, known as blackpoles, were sold for rail and hurdle making. With so much demand for wood, conflicts arose between those wanting standard trees for timber and the tanners who were only interested in bark. Bewdley's last tannery closed in 1928.

Demand for charcoal from the iron industry was cut by its replacement by coal and coke and after World War II demand for the old woodland products declined, so the emphasis was then on forestry, and standard trees rather than coppice growth. In recent years coppicing has revived for amenity reasons as explained in other articles.

Mining

Shropshire has been quite important in the mining of lead, copper, zinc and iron which may well have started in the Bronze Age. But coal was the most important commodity and primitive mines can be dated back to the 13th century.

from Bewdley with flowers

the Severn in Winter

Arley Station

The aqueduct is mainly pipeline but there are 36 miles of tunnels and covered canals. They carry water over 26 rivers or streams including the Wye, Teme and Severn, a canal and a railway. Some of them have deep, steep valleys where the aqueduct takes a dramatic plunge into the depths then shoots up mighty hills. Reservoirs to receive the water were built at Frankley and Bartley Green on the southern edge of Birmingham.

The scheme involved building three main dams retaining over 11,000 million gallons of water. The works required an army of navvies, masons, carpenters, bricklayers and crane drivers, many tons of plant, stones, cement, timber, coal and food. A temporary railway line ran about 3 miles from the Cambrian Railway Company's line through Rhaedaer to the Elan Valley and a village was built. The work took twelve years to complete and cost £6 million.

In the 1950s Birmingham built another dam in the bleak Claerwen Valley to the west of the Elan which retains vastly more water than all the others.

Steam in the Woods

Severn Valley Railway

In 1858 a small railway company built the riverside line to connect the main Worcester to Birmingham railway with Shrewsbury. It was independent until absorbed by the Great Western Railway in 1870. And although the section between Bewdley and Kidderminster looks a natural part of the original route, it was added only in 1878. The new link brought some industrial traffic from the West Midlands but the line carried mainly agricultural freight and coal from mines in the Highley area. It was closed in the Beeching massacre of 1963 and the track north of Bridgnorth was lifted.

The Waterworks

Here and there in the Wyre Forest you will meet broad grass rides which cut straight through the woodland, there are blocky little brick thingys with locked hatches and in some places cemetery style iron railings. Most arresting is the great iron girder bridge set on blue brick arches. All of them are part of the great Elan Valley Aqueduct, a vast scheme opened in 1904 to bring fresh, moorland water from mid Wales to Birmingham.

The 1891 census gave the City's population as 648,000 with a daily water demand of 15 million gallons. This was supplied by five local brooks and five wells. Together they sources were estimated to be good for no more than 20 million gallons per day and their quality was "not beyond reproach". All this water had to be pumped about the City, in some cases three times. The City was exploding with new business and new people and the Corporation could see an imminent water crisis.

Birmingham stands on a plateau above the level of the surrounding land so new sources of water were not easy to find. The most obvious would have been the River Severn but its flow would not have guaranteed sufficient supplies and it would have cost a great deal to pump it up to the City.

In 1890 the Water Committee consulted a distinguished civil engineer, James Mansergh, who recommended that the Corporation buy the 71 square mile catchments of the Rivers Elan and Claerwen to the west of the remote market town of Rhaedaer in mid Wales. This infertile moorland lies on suitable geology, has an annual rainfall of 71 inches and in the late 19th century was occupied by some 300 people. It had one other advantage, this part of mid Wales is higher than Birmingham by 171 feet (about 53 metres), so although it is 74 miles away it would cost nothing to transport the water because it would all flow down by gravity.

115

Until the age of steam, mining was haphazard and small scale. Miners could sink shallow pits, called bell pits, and drive short tunnels from them, or they could drive an "adit" into a hillside. However, when problems of stability, ventilation or flooding arose, and they always did, the workings were abandoned and new ones started. Steam engines allowed water to be pumped from great depths and for miners, roof supports, coal and spoil to be lowered or raised. Thus it was that in the Severn Valley shafts were not sunk until 1870 when work began at Highley.

The first coal was raised in 1878 and working at this pit continued until 1940. In 1936 development work had been shifted across the river to Alveley but the Highley shafts remained in use to ventilate the new mine though a tunnel under the river. Work finally ceased in 1969. The industry has left a great many reminders, not least the typical mining village of Highley. There are theme walk leaflets leading you past the colliery bridge, the rope worked tramway, the railway sidings and various features of the village. Get them from the Visitor Centre. Lying about the valley of the Borle Brook you man see other remnants of old working, an abandoned iron bridge or a rusting truck strangled in the vegetation.

Welsh water over the Severn

The story of the present SVR started in 1965 when the preservation society was formed. Herculean fund raising and engineering efforts by volunteers allowed them to buy and restore sections of the line as cash became available. The Bridgnorth to Hampton Loade section reopened in 1970 and the rest of the line to Bewdley in 1974. The vital link to main line services, between Bewdley and Kidderminster was opened in 1984.

The are stations at Kidderminster, Bewdley, Arley, Highley, Hampton Loade and Bridgnorth, all restored and painted in the cream and ochre GWR colours, with old posters, milk churns, adverts and piles of luggage. Arley Station has won awards for Best Kept Station and been used as a film set. Kidderminster Station is actually new but a well made replica in early 20th century GWR style.

The 15 mile trip includes five viaducts, two tunnels and the beautiful Victoria Bridge over the Severn by Trimpley Reservoir. When built in 1861 by the famous railway contractor, Thomas Brassey, it was the greatest cast iron span in the world. Now it is a graceful monument painted in the GWR buff and ochre. Here photographers have the rare opportunity of snapping a steam train reflected in water. The bridge appeared in a film version of *The Thirty Nine Steps* which starred Robert Powell, where it stood in unconvicingly for a bridge on the North British Railway's east coast main line in wildest Scotland.

The coaches are painted in the liveries of the Great Western Railway (chocolate and cream), London & North Eastern (teak), London, Midland & Scottish (crimson lake) and early British Rail (carmine and cream). They are hauled by a range of finely restored steam engines.

The SVR runs regular trains throughout the year and offers many special services, such as Santa Specials at Christmas, proper dining cars and marriage ceremonies.

The Bewdley to Leominster Railway

This line which crossed the Severn a few yards north of Dowles Brook was built by the Severn Valley Railway in 1861. A tinted photograph of 1864 which you can buy from Bewdley Museum shows a train crossing the new, steel decked bridge. The brick and stone piers are still in place and you can trace the trackbed westward through the forest by a succession of cuttings and embankments. Some of it is now a cycle track but you will have to do some of your tracing on the map because parts are not open to the public.

Photo of Dowles Bridge, 1864

The line followed the valley of Dowles Brook to the old Wyre Forest Station, just south of Furnace Mill, then turned south to a junction at the Blount Arms pub near Cleobury Mortimer. A spur ran to Ditton Priors north of Brown Clee Hill via Stottesdon, Aston Botterell and Cleobury North, a railway trying to get away from it all and commit commercial suicide. In fact it served a naval amunition dump so the seclusion was reasonable.

From Blount Arms the main line ran on through Neen Sollars, Newnham Bridge and Tenbury Wells to Woofferton (that's right), where it joined the main Hereford to Shrewsbury line. What a wistful, rural idyll, rolling up Edward Thomas's *Adlestrop* and that vision of pastoral England from Flanders and Swann's song *The Slow Train*. Not surprisingly it never made money, but good heavens, perhaps the great station master in the sky never intended it to. The unsympathetic Dr Beeching did not understand this view so the line was closed in 1961 and the track raised a couple of years later.